Experimenting with Plants Science Projects

Robert Gardner

Enslow Publishers, Inc.
40 Industrial Road
Box 398
Berkeley Heights, NJ 07922
USA
http://www.enslow.com

Original edition published as *Science Projects About Plants* in 1999.

Library of Congress Cataloging-in-Publication Data

Gardner, Robert, 1929–
    [Science projects about plants]
    Experimenting with plants science projects / Robert Gardner.
       p. cm.–(Exploring hands-on science projects)
    Previously published as: Science projects about plants. c1999.
    Summary: "Learn the science behind plant physiology, reproduction and growth"–
Provided by publisher.
    Includes bibliographical references and index.
    ISBN 978-0-7660-4144-8
    1. Botany projects–Juvenile literature. 2. Plants–Experiments–Juvenile literature. I. Title.
    QK52.6.G37 2013
    580–dc23

                    2012010123

Future editions:
Paperback ISBN: 978-1-4644-0220-3
Single-User PDF ISBN: 978-1-4646-1133-9

EPUB ISBN: 978-1-4645-1133-2
Multi-User PDF ISBN: 978-0-7660-5762-3

Printed in China

012013 Leo Paper Group, Heshan City, Guangdong, China

10 9 8 7 6 5 4 3 2 1

To Our Readers: We have done our best to make sure all Internet addresses in this book were active
and appropriate when we went to press. However, the author and the publisher have no control
over and assume no liability for the material available on those Internet sites or on other Web sites
they may link to. Any comments or suggestions can be sent by e-mail to comments@enslow.com or
to the address on the back cover.

Contents

Indicates experiments that offer ideas for science fair projects.

Indicates experiments that offer ideas for science fair projects.

INTRODUCTION

The science projects and experiments in this book have to do with plants. For some of the experiments you will need more than one pair of hands. In those cases ask friends or family members to help you. Since some of the experiments will take some time, try to choose friends who are patient. It might be best if you work with someone or some others who enjoy experimenting with plants as much as you do. In a few experiments where there is a potential for danger, you will be asked to work with an adult. Please do so! We do not want you to take any chances that could lead to an injury.

As you do these projects, you will find it useful to record in a notebook your ideas, notes, data, and anything you can conclude from your experiments. In that way, you can keep track of the information you gather and the conclusions you reach. You can use your notebook to refer to other experiments you have done, which may help you in doing future projects.

SCIENCE FAIRS

Some of the projects in this book might be appropriate for a science fair. Those projects are indicated with an asterisk (*). However, judges at such fairs do not reward projects or experiments that are simply copied from a book. For example, a model of a flower, which is commonly found at these fairs, would probably not impress judges unless it was done in a novel or creative way. On the other hand, a model of a flower that showed in smooth flowing sequence what happens inside a flower during pollination, fertilization, and the subsequent development of seeds and surrounding fruit would receive more consideration than a rigid papier-mâché model.

Science fair judges tend to reward creative thought and imagination. However, it's difficult to be creative or imaginative unless you are really interested in your project, so choose something that appeals to you. Consider, too, your own ability and the cost of materials needed for the project. Don't pursue a project that you can't afford or one that doesn't interest you.

If you decide to use a project found in this book for a science fair, you'll need to find ways to modify or extend the project. This should not be difficult because you'll probably find that as you do these projects new ideas for experiments will come to mind. These new experiments could make excellent science fair projects, particularly because they spring from your own mind and are interesting to you.

If you decide to enter a science fair and have never done so before, you should read some of the books listed in the "Further Reading". The references that deal specifically with science fairs will provide plenty of helpful hints and lots of useful information that will enable you to avoid the pitfalls that sometimes plague first-time entrants. You'll learn how to prepare appealing reports that include charts and graphs, how to set up and display your work, how to present your project, and how to relate to judges and visitors.

SAFETY FIRST

Most of the projects included in this book are perfectly safe. However, the following safety rules are well worth reading before you start any project.

1. Do any experiments or projects, whether from this book or of your own design, under the supervision of a science teacher or other knowledgeable adult.
2. Read all instructions carefully before proceeding with a project. If you have questions, check with your supervisor before going any further.
3. Maintain a serious attitude while conducting experiments. Fooling around can be dangerous to you and to others.
4. Wear approved safety goggles when you are doing anything that might cause injury to your eyes.
5. Do not eat or drink while experimenting.
6. Have a first-aid kit nearby while you are experimenting.
7. Do not put your fingers or any object in electrical outlets.
8. Never experiment with household electricity except under the supervision of a knowledgeable adult.
9. Do not touch a lit high-wattage bulb. Lightbulbs produce light, but they also produce heat.
10. Never look directly at the sun. It can cause permanent damage to your eyes.

The Scientific Method

How Scientists Search for Answers

When scientists have a question to answer, they start by researching. They read scientific literature and consult online science databases that are maintained by universities, research centers, or the government. There, they can study abstracts—summaries of reports—by scientists who have conducted experiments or done similar research in the field.

In this way, they find out whether other scientists have examined the same question or have tried to answer it by doing an experiment. Careful research will tell what kind of experiments, if any, have been done to try to answer the question.

Scientists don't want to repeat experiments that have known and accepted outcomes. Also, they want to avoid repeating any mistakes others may have made while doing similar experiments. If no one else has done scientific work that answers the question, scientists then do further research on how best to do the experiment.

While researching for the experiment, the scientist tries to guess—or predict—the possible results. This prediction is called a hypothesis.

The scientist hopes that a well-researched and carefully planned experiment will prove the hypothesis to be true. At times, however, the results of even the best-planned experiment can be far different from what the scientist expected. Yet even if the results indicate the hypothesis was not true, this does not mean the experiment was a failure. In fact, unexpected results can provide valuable information that leads to a different answer or to another, even better, experiment.

Using the Scientific Method in Experiments and Projects
The Scientific Method

A scientific experiment starts when someone wonders what would happen if certain conditions were set up and tested by following a specific process. For example, in an experiment testing the ability of table salt (sodium chloride) to conduct electricity, you can ask the question: "Is table salt more conductive when it is dissolved in water to make a saltwater solution?"

To find the answer, some possible guesses, hypotheses, would be:

- Solid table salt conducts electricity better than saltwater.
- Saltwater conducts electricity better than solid table salt.
- Neither form of table salt will conduct electricity.

Let's say your hypothesis is that salt water will conduct electricity better than the solid table salt. For a start, we have to know that a scientific experiment can have only two variables— that is, only two things that can change. For this experiment, one variable is whether the salt is dissolved in water or whether it is solid. The other variable will be the electrical conductivity of each form of salt.

The form of salt is allowed to change (either a solid or in solution) but not the equipment producing the electrical charge, and not the amount or strength of the charge the equipment produces. If the electrical charge differed when the solid salt and the salt solution were tested, then we couldn't tell how the conductivity of one form compared to the other.

Now, if the experiment is carried out and the results show there is no difference in the conductivity of solid salt and dissolved salt, this would not mean your experiment is a failure. Even if your hypothesis—dissolved salt conducts electricity better—turns out to be false, the results of your experiment still can provide important information. And these results may lead to further ideas that can be explored.

Scientists may develop logical explanations for the results of their experiments. These explanations, or theories, then must be tested by more experiments. If the resulting data from more experiments provide compelling support for a theory, then that theory could be accepted by the world of science. But scientists are careful about accepting new theories. If the resulting data contradict a theory, then the theory must be discarded, altered, or retested. That is the scientific method.

Basic Steps in the Scientific Method

The best experiments and science projects usually follow the scientific method's basic steps:

- Ask questions about what would happen if certain conditions or events were set up and tested in an experiment.
- Do background research to investigate the subject of your questions until you have a main question.
- Construct a hypothesis—an answer to your question—that you can then test and investigate with an experiment.
- Design and conduct an experiment to test your hypothesis.
- Keep records, collecting data, and then analyze what you've recorded.
- Draw a conclusion based on the experiment and the data you've recorded.
- Write a report about your results.

Your Hypothesis

Many experiments and science projects begin by asking whether something can be done or how it can be done. How do you search for an answer? Form your hypothesis? First, read about your topic. After your research, you might make an educated guess in answer to the question; this is your hypothesis. You'll also find out what methods, materials, and equipment are needed to design an experiment that tests your hypothesis.

Remember: To give your experiment or project every chance of success, prepare a hypothesis that is clear and brief. The simpler the better.

Designing the Experiment

Your experiment will be structured to investigate whether the hypothesis is true or false. The experiment is intended to test the hypothesis, not necessarily to prove that the hypothesis is right.

The results of a well-designed experiment are more valuable than the results of an experiment that is intentionally designed to give the answer you want. The conditions you set up in your experiment must be a fair test of your hypothesis.

By carefully carrying out your experiment you'll discover useful information that can be recorded as data (observations). It's most important that the experiment's procedures and results are as accurate as possible. Design the experiment for observable, measurable results. And keep it simple, because the more complicated your experiment is, the more chance you have for error.

Also, if you have friends helping you with an experiment or project, make sure from the start that they'll take their tasks seriously.

Remember: Scientists around the world always use metric measurements in their experiments and projects, and so should you. Use metric liquid and dry measures and a Celsius thermometer.

Recording Data

Your hypothesis, procedure, data, and conclusions should be recorded immediately as you experiment, but don't keep it on loose scraps of paper. Record your data in a notebook or logbook—one you use just for experiments. Your notebook should be bound so that you have a permanent record. The laboratory notebook is an essential part of all academic and scientific research.

Make sure to include the date, experiment number, and a brief description of how you collected the data. Write clearly. If you have to cross something out, do it with just a single line, then rewrite the correct information.

Repeat your experiment several times to be sure your results are consistent and your data are trustworthy. Don't try to interpret data as you go along. It's better first to record results accurately, then study them later.

You might even find that you want to replace your experiment's original question with a new one. For example, by answering the question, "What is the chemical process behind yeast as a leavening agent?" you learn that yeast consumes sugar (glucose).This brings up other questions: "Is there a limit to how much sugar yeast can digest? Can too much sugar inhibit the leavening process?"

Writing the Science Fair Report

Communicate the results of your experiment by writing a clear report. Even the most successful experiment loses its value if the scientist cannot clearly tell what happened. Your report should describe how the experiment was designed and conducted and should state its precise results.

Following are the parts of a science fair report, in the order they should appear:

• The Title Page

The title of your experiment should be centered and near the top of the page. Your teacher will tell you what other information is needed, such as your name, grade, and the name of your science teacher.

- **Table of Contents**

On the report's second page, list the remaining parts of the report and their page numbers.

- **Abstract**

Give a brief overview of your experiment. In just a few sentences, tell the purpose of the experiment, what you did, and what you found out. Always write in plain, clear language.

- **Introduction**

State your hypothesis and explain how you came up with it. Discuss your experiment's main question and how your research led to the hypothesis. Tell what you hoped to achieve when you started the experiment.

- **Experiment and Data**

This is a detailed step-by-step explanation of how you organized and carried out the experiment. Explain what methods you followed and what materials and equipment you used.

State when the experiment was done (the date and perhaps the time of day) and under what conditions (in a laboratory, outside on a windy day, in cold or warm weather, etc.) Tell who was involved and what part they played in the experiment.

Include clearly labeled graphs and tables of data from the experiment as well as any photographs or drawings that help illustrate your work. Anyone who reads your report should be able to repeat the experiment just the way you did it. (Repeating an experiment is a good way to test whether the original results were obtained correctly.)

- **Discussion**

Explain your results and conclusions, perhaps comparing them with published scientific data you first read about in your research. Consider how the experiment's results relate to your hypothesis. Ask yourself: Do my results support or contradict my hypothesis? Then analyze the answer.

Would you do anything differently if you did this experiment again? State what you've learned as a result of the experiment.

Analyze how your tools and equipment did their tasks, and how well you and others used those tools. If you think the experiment could be done better if designed another way or if you've another hypothesis that might be tested, then include this in your discussion.

• Conclusion

Make a brief summary of your experiment's results. Include only information and data already stated in the report, and be sure not to bring in any new information.

• Acknowledgments

Give credit to everyone who helped you with the experiment. State the names of these individuals and briefly explain who they are and how they assisted you.

• References / Bibliography

List any books, magazines, journals, articles, Web sites, scientific databases, and interviews that were important to your research for the experiment.

Science Fairs

Science fair judges tend to reward creative thought and imagination. It's difficult to be creative or imaginative unless you're really interested in your project. So, be sure to choose a subject that appeals to you. And before you jump into a project, consider your own talents and the cost of materials you'll need.

Remember, judges at science fairs don't reward projects or experiments that are simply copied from a book. If you decide to use a project from this book for a science fair, you should find ways to modify or extend it. This shouldn't be difficult because you'll probably discover that, as you do these projects, new ideas for experiments will come to mind. These experiments could make excellent science fair projects, particularly because the ideas are your own and are interesting to you.

If you decide to enter a science fair and have never done so before, you should read some of the books listed in the Further Reading section and visit the Internet sites. The books and sites with titles that refer to science fairs will provide plenty of helpful hints and information that will help you avoid the pitfalls that sometimes plague first-time entrants. You'll learn how to prepare appealing reports that include charts and graphs, how to set up and display your work, how to present your project, and how to relate to judges and visitors. Following are some suggestions to consider.

Some Tips for Success at a Science Fair

Science teachers and science fair judges have many different opinions on what makes a good science fair project or experiment.

Here are the most important elements:

Originality of Concept is one of the most important things judges consider. Some judges believe that the best science fair projects answer a question that is not found in a science textbook.

Scientific Content is another main area of evaluation. How was science applied in the procedure? Are there sufficient data? Did you stick to your intended procedure and keep good records?

Thoroughness is next in importance. Was the experiment repeated as often as needed to test your hypothesis? Is your notebook complete, and are the data accurate? Does your research bibliography show you did enough library work?

Clarity in how you present your exhibit shows you had a good understanding of the subject you worked on. It's important that your exhibit clearly presents the results of your work.

Effective Process: Judges recognize that how skillfully you carry out a science fair project is usually more important than its results. A well-done project gives students the best understanding of what scientists actually do day-to-day.

Other points to consider when preparing for your science fair:

The Abstract: Write up a brief explanation of your project and make copies for visitors or judges who want to read it.

Knowledge: Be ready to answer questions from visitors and judges confidently. Know what is in your notebook and make some notes on index cards to remind you of important points.

Practice: Before the science fair begins, prepare a list of several questions you think you might be asked. Think about the answers and about how your display can help to support them. Have a friend or parent ask you questions and answer them out loud. Knowing your work thoroughly helps you feel more confident when you're asked about it.

Appearance: Dress and act in a way that shows you take your project seriously. Visitors and judges should get the impression that you're interested in the project and take pride in answering their questions about it.

Remember: Don't block your exhibit. Stand to the side when someone is looking at it.

Some projects have special needs with respect to displays. If you cannot show the experiment or results, photograph or draw them. Show the materials used at the start of the experiment and those produced at the end, if possible, and mount them on a display. Photograph or draw any special tools or setups. Be inventive about different ways of showing what took place.

Chapter 1

Experimenting with Seeds

Seeds are part of the life cycle of many of the green plants with which we are most familiar. Under the right conditions seeds germinate and grow into mature plants that produce flowers or cones. The flowers or cones produce egg and sperm cells that join to form embryo plants. In plants such as pine trees, the naked seeds fall from their cones, but in other plants, particularly those we call vegetables or fruit, the seeds are surrounded by the ripened ovaries (fruit) of the flowers in which fertilization took place. When the fruit opens, is eaten, or decays, the seeds may fall on soil where they can germinate and the cycle begins all over again. In many cases, seed companies collect the seeds, possibly treat them to increase their chances of germination, and then package and sell them to farmers or people who enjoy gardening or growing much of their own food.

Whether plant life began with the seed or the plant is similar to the age-old question: Which came first, the chicken or the egg? Certainly, the seed marks a distinct point in the life cycle of plants and so we will begin there by experimenting with seeds.

1.1 Collecting Seeds

Materials:
- seeds from a wide variety of sources

Although the seeds of any given plant look very much alike, they do differ significantly in size. The seeds of various species are very different in appearance as well. To see the many ways that seeds differ, you can collect the seeds of various species of plants.

Beans, peas, and kernels of corn that you buy in a grocery store as food are actually seeds produced by plants with the same names. We eat many seeds—beans, peas, corn, peanuts, barley, and others. Other foods in the store, such as squash, pumpkins, tomatoes, peppers, and other plants, have seeds, too, but they are inside the vegetables. Seeds we do not eat can be found in many of the fruits we eat—oranges, apples, cantaloupes, grapefruit, peaches, plums, and grapes, all contain seeds that you can collect and save. Nuts, such as acorns, horse chestnuts, and beechnuts, can be found in abundance beneath oak, horse chestnut, and beech trees come autumn. The seeds of locust and catalpa trees are inside long pods that hang from the trees in late summer. Some trees, such as maples, produce seeds with wings. After they dry, their wings spin like helicopter blades as they fall. The wind may carry them far from the tree that produced them. All the seeds mentioned above are found in the fruit that begins as part of a plant's flower.

Not all seeds come from the fruit that develops in a flower. If you look closely, you can find seeds in pine cones that have matured and are no longer green.

Milkweed and dandelions produce seeds with fluffy hairs. The wind will carry these seeds over great distances. Can you find other seeds with structures that allow the wind to distribute them over a wide area?

Collect as many seeds as you can. Try to identify the seeds you collect by noting the plants, trees, or fruit from which they came. If you wish, small drops of glue can be used to attach the seeds to poster paper or cardboard. Identifying labels with sticky backs can be placed beside the seeds.

How many different kinds of seeds can you find in a supermarket? Will any of these seeds germinate if you plant them in soil? Will they germinate if you wrap them in moist paper towels?

1.2 A Look at Seeds

Materials:
- lima beans or red kidney beans (you can buy a small bag of these seeds at a grocery store or supermarket)
- water
- 2 drinking glasses
- paper towels
- plastic dish or small cardboard box lined with plastic
- cover for container
- corn seeds
- adult supervisor
- sharp knife
- forceps

A seed is basically an embryo plant with the stored food it needs wrapped in a protective coat called the testa. Food needed to nourish the embryo plant is stored in cells that make up the endosperm. The first small leaves of the plant are the cotyledons. In some plants, such as beans, peas, and pumpkins whose seeds germinate quickly after planting, the endosperm is absorbed by the embryo before the seeds are shed. In other plants, such as corn, oats, and wheat, the embryo plants do not digest and absorb the food stored in the endosperm until after the seeds are planted and take in water. These seeds tend to take longer to germinate because the embryos have to absorb food from the endosperm before they can begin vigorous growth.

Look at a few lima beans or red kidney beans. These are large seeds that we eat. They are easier to examine than smaller seeds. Can you find the parts shown in Figure 1?

[FIGURE 1]

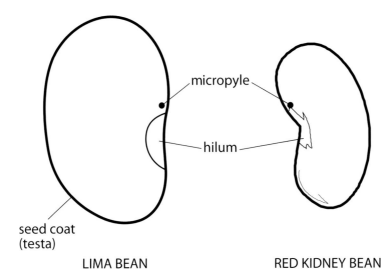

micropyle

hilum

seed coat
(testa)

LIMA BEAN   RED KIDNEY BEAN

Exteriors of two large seeds. The drawings of a lima bean seed and a red kidney bean seed show the hilum and micropyle. The hilum is a scar that marks the region where the seed was attached to the pod (fruit) from which it came. The tiny micropyle is a hole through which the pollen tube grew before the egg within the ovule was fertilized. Seeds are covered by a seed coat (testa) that protects the tiny embryo plant and reduces the evaporation of water from the seed.

Soak a dozen of these seeds overnight in a glass of water. The water will soften the seed coat. Leave another dozen in a glass that has no water. After about twenty-four hours, examine both sets of seeds. How do they differ? How does the volume of the dry seeds compare with the volume of the seeds that soaked overnight?

Working over a paper towel, carefully remove the softened seed coat from one of the seeds that was in water. You'll find a seam on the convex (rounded) side of the bean. Gently slide a fingernail into that seam and

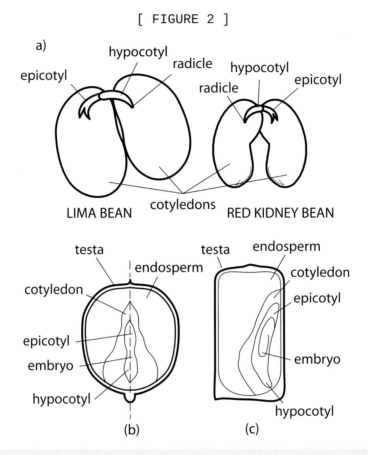

[FIGURE 2]

a)

epicotyl — hypocotyl — radicle — hypocotyl — epicotyl — radicle

LIMA BEAN — cotyledons — RED KIDNEY BEAN

testa — endosperm — testa — endosperm — cotyledon — epicotyl

cotyledon — epicotyl — embryo — hypocotyl — embryo — hypocotyl

(b) (c)

a) Interiors of two large seeds. Here are two kinds of bean seeds that have been opened to reveal the tiny embryos within. The small leafy structure is the epicotyl. It becomes the plant's first true leaves. The tougher, thicker part of the embryo is the hypocotyl. The lower end of the hypocotyl (the radicle) becomes the plant's primary root. The lower part of the epicotyl and the upper part of the hypocotyl become the plant's stem. The large cotyledons, which make up most of a bean seed's volume, contain stored food that was absorbed from the endosperm. b) A corn seed with its seed coat (testa) stripped off the front, wide, flat side of the seed. c) A corn seed cut in half across its narrow side.

separate the two large cotyledons (seed leaves) that make up most of the bean seed. If you have worked carefully, you will see a tiny embryo plant like the one shown in Figure 2a. Can you identify the epicotyl and hypocotyl?

Repeat the experiment with corn seeds (kernels) that have soaked overnight. Use forceps to carefully strip off the seed coat. Look at the flat side of the seed that is white and badge shaped. Can you see the structures shown in Figure 2b? **Under adult supervision**, use a sharp knife to cut the seed in half. Cut along the dotted line shown in the drawing. Now turn the seed 90 degrees. You should be able to see the structures shown in Figure 2c.

As you can see, a corn seed is quite different from a lima bean seed. Its embryo is very small, it has but one cotyledon, and the endosperm has not been digested and absorbed by the embryo.

EXPLORING ON YOUR OWN

Can you germinate any of the seeds you collected in Experiment 1.1? Can you plant any of them in soil and grow new plants?

Materials:
- lima beans (you can buy a small bag of these seeds at a grocery store or supermarket)
- balance
- graduated cylinder or a metric measuring cup
- water
- paper towels
- saucer or small dish
- plastic container that fits over the saucer or dish

Imbibed water is water that is absorbed or drunk. In this experiment you will determine the water imbibed by bean seeds. Put about a dozen lima bean seeds on a balance pan. What is the mass of the dry seeds, in grams (g)? On the basis of the weighing, how much does an average bean seed weigh?

To find the volume of these bean seeds, drop them into a graduated cylinder or a metric measuring cup that contains 50 mL of water. What is the water level after the beans are added? What does that make the volume of the bean seeds? What is the average volume of a bean seed?

How can you find the density of the bean seeds; that is, their mass per volume? How does it compare with the density of water, which is 1.0 g/mL?

Let the beans soak in water overnight. After about 24 hours, remove the beans from the water. Dry them by patting them gently with paper towels and then weigh them again. How much water, in grams, did the beans imbibe? What was the average amount of water imbibed by a bean seed?

Save one or two of the soaked bean seeds for the next experiment. Drop four or five bean seeds back into a container of water. Place a similar number on a folded paper towel that fits on a saucer or small dish. Add enough water to make the towel moist and cover it with an inverted plastic container that fits over the saucer or dish. Do the seeds on the paper towel germinate after a few days? Do the seeds that are under water germinate? Do you notice anything else about the seeds that were under water?

1.4 Stored Food

Materials:

- lima bean seeds (you can buy a small bag of these seeds at a grocery store or supermarket)
- water
- plastic wrap
- table or counter
- spoon
- iodine (tincture of iodine can be purchased at a drugstore)
- corn seeds
- adult supervisor
- knife
- paper towels

Soak a lima bean seed and a corn seed overnight. Remove the seed coat from the lima bean seed and put the seed coat on a sheet of plastic wrap. Add a drop of iodine to the seed coat. **Iodine is poisonous! Never put it in your mouth. Wash your hands when you are finished!** Use a spoon to rub the iodine into the seed coat. If there is starch in the seed coat, it will react with the iodine to form a blue-black color after a short time. Does the seed coat contain starch?

Remove one of the cotyledons from the bean seed and place it on the plastic sheet. Use the spoon to mash (break up and squash) the cotyledon. Then add a drop of the iodine solution and watch. Does the cotyledon contain starch?

Place a corn seed that has soaked overnight on the plastic sheet. **Under adult supervision**, cut the seed in half. Use the knife to break up the contents of the seed's endosperm. Then add a drop of the iodine solution. Does the corn seed contain starch?

To see why you were asked to place the seeds on plastic rather than a paper towel, fold a piece of paper towel. Then add a drop of iodine solution to the towel. What happens? Does the paper towel contain starch?

Materials:

- coleus plants in pots
- large, sharp nail
- plastic dishpan about 20 cm (8 in) deep x 30 cm (12 in) on a side
- facial tissue
- sand, Vermiculite, or Perlite
- water
- coat hangers
- large transparent plastic bag
- large rubber band or several smaller ones strung together with paper clips
- adult supervisor
- sharp knife
- ivy, philodendrons, African violets, begonias, geraniums
- young bean plants
- 500-mL (1-pint) jar
- salt
- sugar
- boric acid
- teaspoon
- thermometer

In 1996, scientists in Scotland succeeded in cloning a sheep. That is, a ewe (female sheep) produced a lamb that would grow into an adult identical in every way to its mother because it carried the same "package" of genes as its mother. While this was the first time anyone had succeeded in cloning a mammal, plants have been cloned for centuries. For many plants, cloning is one of the ways they reproduce.

Seeds are necessary to produce variations in plants because seeds contain embryos. The embryos carry genes that came from the sperm cells of a pollen grain from another plant's stamen as well as the egg within the pistil of the plant that holds the seed. (See Figure 23 on page 99.) Plant pollination is described on page 81.

To produce plants by cloning, sometimes called rooting, buy two or three coleus plants from a gardening store or greenhouse. Then make a cloning bed where the plants can grow. You can do this by first using a large, sharp nail to punch a few holes in the bottom of a plastic dishpan that is about 20 cm (8 in) deep and 30 cm (12 in) on a side. Wiggle the nail around in each hole to make it wide so that water will drain out of the pan and not rot the roots as they develop.

Before you add sand to the pan, cover the holes with facial tissue. The tissue will prevent grains of sand from falling out but will allow water to drain away. Add about 15 cm (6 in) of sand to the pan. If you can't obtain sand, use Vermiculite or Perlite, which can be purchased at a garden store. Put the pan in a sink or outdoors on concrete or stones. Pour about half a liter (1 pint) of water over the sand and let any excess drain through the pan. Add more water if necessary to make the sand damp throughout. Put the bed of sand in a warm, light area but not in direct sunlight.

Next, you will need to build a transparent cover for the bed to reduce water loss and provide humid air around the plants. You can make a frame out of coat hangers as shown in Figure 3a. A sheet cut from a large transparent plastic bag can be placed over the frame. Use a large rubber band or several smaller ones strung together with paper clips to hold the sheet in place.

Under adult supervision, use a sharp knife to cut off a coleus plant about 5 to 8 cm (2–3 in) above the soil in which it is growing. Trim away the small lower leaves to make a stem that looks like the one shown in Figure 3b.

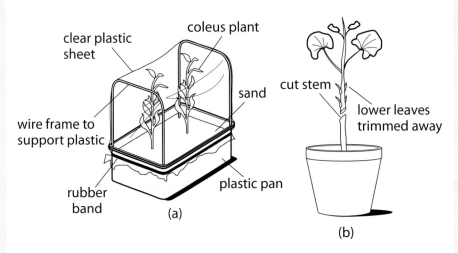

[FIGURE 3]

a) A bed of sand in a plastic pan with a clear plastic cover is a good place to clone plants. b) A coleus plant is cut and then stuck in a bed of moist sand.

Now stick the plant's stem into the sand. Do the same for another one or two coleus plants. Then replace the plastic sheet.

Keep the pots containing the stumps of the plants from which you made the cuttings. Continue to water these pots. Do the stumps give rise to new leaves?

Lift the plastic cover over the cuttings you placed in sand every other day and feel the sand. If it is dry add a cup of water. If it is damp, simply replace the cover. After about three weeks, gently pull upward on the stem of one of the plants in the sand. If it moves easily, leave it for another week. If it is firmly held in the sand, you can assume roots have formed. In that case, use a kitchen knife or garden trowel to cut around the roots and remove the plant from the sand. Transfer the plant to a pot that contains potting soil. You have cloned the original plant from which you cut the stem.

Try to clone ivy (not the poisonous kind) and philodendrons. Some people claim that African violets can be cloned by simply immersing the petiole (stem) of a leaf in moist sand. Try rooting an African violet leaf by sticking the petiole of one of its leaves into moist soil. Does it form roots and grow into a new plant like its parent? Can you clone begonias and geraniums? Try cloning a number of other plants. Which ones can be cloned? Which plants were you unable to clone? Do some research to find out whether or not people have succeeded in cloning plants that you could not clone. Perhaps they used special techniques that you can use to root these plants as well.

Try cloning young bean plants by placing the cut stems of four or five of them with leaves attached in a 500-mL (1-pint) jar of water. You might also try solutions of salt, sugar, and boric acid. Prepare the solutions by dissolving about 1/8 teaspoon of the solid in 500 mL (1 pint) of water. Add a teaspoonful of the solution you are testing to a pint of the water in which you placed the bean plants. Do any of the solutions affect the rate at which the plants develop roots?

EXPLORING ON YOUR OWN

Develop a hypothesis to explain how you think temperature will affect the rate at which cuttings develop roots. Then design and carry out an experiment to check your hypothesis. Was your hypothesis correct or did you have to modify it?

Chapter 2

Germinating Seeds

Although many seeds will germinate as soon as they receive water and are in warm temperatures, others will sprout only after they pass through a resting stage known as dormancy. For many plants dormancy is an adaptation for survival. In climates that have cold winters, seedlings would soon die if they germinated during the autumn soon after they fell from the parent plants. By remaining dormant during months of cold weather, their chances of survival improve dramatically.

Often seeds that pass through a dormant period have hard thick coats through which water cannot pass. They may have to be nicked in some way before water can enter the seed and induce germination. The nicking can be caused by natural forces such as freezing and thawing, bacteria, or other factors. For seeds of significant agricultural importance, such as clover, machines with abrasive devices are used to scar their seed coats so that they will germinate when sown in moist soil.

The viability of seeds, or their ability to germinate, is lost after a period of time. Yet the period during which seeds are viable varies considerably. The seeds of some willows are viable for only a few days, while four-hundred-year-old Indian lotus seeds have germinated after being nicked and provided with moisture and warmth. Most seeds are viable for no more than ten years. Seeds stored under cool, dry conditions will retain their viability longer than those stored in a warm, damp environment. Other seeds are dormant because certain slow chemical reactions must take place within them before they are ready to germinate.

2.1 Watching Seeds Germinate

Materials:
- paper towels
- seeds—lima bean, navy bean, radish, corn, lentil, peas, and others
- large, clear drinking glass
- newspaper

You can watch seeds in a glass germinate in much the same way that they would in soil. Line the walls of a large drinking glass with several paper towels as shown in Figure 4. Wet the towels so they will stick to the glass. Fill the rest of the glass with a crumpled sheet of newspaper. The newspaper will hold the towels in place. Pour water into the bottom of the glass until it is about 2 to 3 cm (1 in) deep. Capillary action will carry the water up the paper towel to keep it wet.

Now you are ready to "plant" the seeds. Place different kinds of seeds, several of each kind, between the moist towels and the glass. You might include corn, lima beans, and any others that are available. Orient the seeds in different ways—upside down, right side up, and sideways. Prepare as many paper-towel-lined glasses as you wish.

How long does it take each kind of seed to germinate? Keep careful records. Which seeds germinate first? Which germinate last? Watch the seedlings after they have germinated. Do all the seedlings grow straight up? What happens when a seed is planted with its embryo's hypocotyl above its epicotyl? What happens if its epicotyl and hypocotyl are at the same level? Can seeds that germinate in your "observatorium" be transplanted to soil and survive?

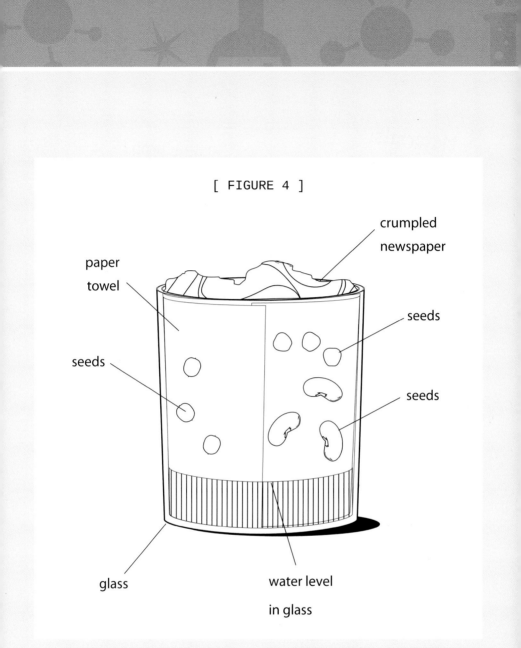

[FIGURE 4]

crumpled
newspaper

paper
towel

seeds

seeds

seeds

glass

water level
in glass

With a setup like this you can watch seeds germinate as they would in soil. Does their orientation affect their germination?

Materials:
- wide, shallow trays
- paper towels
- seeds—lima bean, navy bean, radish, corn, lentil, peas, and others
- plastic wrap
- stick-on labels
- refrigerator
- dark room or closet

Germinating seeds reveal the emergence of life from something that was previously dormant and seemingly lifeless. In this experiment you will find what is needed to change an apparently inert seed into a growing seedling.

Cover the bottoms of four large shallow trays with two or three layers of paper towels. In three of the trays dampen (don't soak) the towels with water. Place about a dozen seeds of each kind you want to germinate in separate regions on the towels in each tray. Then cover the trays with clear plastic wrap. Leave one end of the plastic loose so air can reach the seeds. The clear plastic covers will reduce the rate at which water evaporates from the towels while still allowing you to observe the seeds.

Apply stick-on labels to the plastic wrap so you can identify the seeds in the trays. Place one of the trays with damp towels in a refrigerator. Leave two trays, one with damp towels, one with dry towels in a warm room. Place another tray with damp towels in a warm, dark room or closet. Check the seeds each day and add enough water to keep the damp towels moist. Add no water to the tray with the dry towel.

After watching the seeds for a few days, see if you can answer the following questions. Can seeds germinate without being placed in soil? Is water essential for germination? Does temperature affect germination? If it does, how does it affect germination? Is light or darkness essential for seeds to germinate? Is either light or darkness essential for some kinds of seeds to germinate? Which seeds germinate quickly? Which seeds take a long time to germinate?

EXPLORING ON YOUR OWN

Design an experiment to find out whether or not pea seeds will germinate in colder temperatures than corn seeds. Will the birdseed you buy in a store germinate?

If the birdseed germinates, will it germinate in a refrigerator? Will it germinate in a freezer?

2.3 Air and Germination

In Experiment 2.2 you found that certain conditions involving temperature, light, and water are needed for seeds to germinate. In all those experiments all the seeds had air regardless of the temperature, moisture, and light conditions. In this experiment you will prevent air from reaching seeds by covering them with a thin layer of petroleum jelly.

To begin, soak a dozen bean seeds in water overnight. Dry the seeds with a paper towel. Then spread petroleum jelly over the surface of half the seeds. Place these seeds on a layer of damp paper towels. Add a similar number of bean seeds that are not covered with petroleum jelly to a second layer of damp paper towels. Fold the towels over both sets of seeds and place them side by side in a wide shallow tray. Place the tray in a warm room and cover it with plastic wrap to reduce the rate that water evaporates from the towels.

Examine the seeds daily. Do the seeds that are coated with petroleum jelly germinate at the same time as the regular seeds? Do both sets of seeds eventually germinate?

2.4 More on Air and Germination

Materials:

- 18 bean seeds
- potting or garden soil
- 3 clear plastic or glass jars with screw-on caps
- water
- adult supervisor
- stove to boil water

Critics could argue that the coated bean seeds in the previous experiment did not germinate because the petroleum jelly prevented water from reaching the seeds. Perhaps water is needed outside as well as inside for the seeds to germinate.

In this experiment you will plant 6 bean seeds in soil in each of 3 clear plastic or glass jars. Fill the jars about halfway with soil. In the first jar place dry soil. Put damp soil in the second and third jars. Push the seeds into the soil along the walls of the jars. In that way you will be able to see the seeds. Keep the soil in the second jar damp by adding water as needed. **Under adult supervision**, boil and cool some water. Add it to the third jar to cover the seeds in the soil. Boiling the water removes most of the air dissolved in it. Seal the third jar by screwing on the lid so that additional air cannot reach the seeds.

Which, if any, of the seeds do you think will germinate? Why do you think so? Observe the seeds over the next few days. Did you predict correctly?

After two weeks, try adding water to the dry soil. Will the seeds germinate after water is provided? Open the sealed jar. What do you notice about the odor? Can you explain what has happened?

EXPLORING ON YOUR OWN

Air is a mixture of primarily nitrogen (78 percent) and oxygen (21 percent). The remaining one percent is made up of argon, carbon dioxide, water vapor, and other gases. **Under the supervision of a knowledgeable adult**, try to find out which of the gases that make up air are needed by seeds in order to germinate.

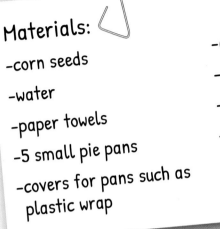

2.5 Germinating Seeds and Freezing Temperatures

Materials:
- corn seeds
- water
- paper towels
- 5 small pie pans
- covers for pans such as plastic wrap
- a freezer
- masking tape
- marking pen
- warm room
- bean, radish, mustard, and other seeds

What effect will freezing temperatures—temperatures below 0°C or 32°F—have on germinating seeds at different stages of their development? To find out, place a few corn seeds on some wet paper towels in a small pie pan. Cover the pan loosely so that evaporation is reduced but air can still reach the seeds. Allow the seeds to germinate for about a week, adding water if necessary, until the seedlings are about one centimeter tall. A day later you will put the pan and seedlings into a freezer. But during that 24-hour period, prepare four other pans of corn seeds. One pan should contain seeds that have soaked in water for 24 hours. A second pan should have seeds that have been on the wet towels for 18 hours. A third, a fourth, and a fifth pan should have seeds that have rested on the wet towels for six, three, and one hour respectively. Use masking tape and a marking pen to label the pans according to the number of hours the seeds have been absorbing water.

At the appropriate time (1 hour after the seeds were added to the fifth pan) place the pans with the seeds on the towels in a freezer and leave them there for 24 hours. Remove all the pans at that time and leave them in a warm room. Add water if necessary to be sure the seeds are resting on moist towels. Which, if any, of the seeds continue to germinate or grow? Can you draw any conclusions from the results of your experiment?

EXPLORING ON YOUR OWN

You might like to repeat the experiment with germination at freezing temperatures using other kinds of seeds. You might try bean, radish, mustard, and other seeds. How do your results for different types of seeds compare? Which, if any seeds, germinate at freezing temperatures?

Materials:

- 8 wide, shallow trays
- paper towels
- 400 radish seeds
- plastic wrap
- dark closet or other darkplace
- thermometer

Some seeds must be exposed to light before they will germinate; other seeds become dormant in light. Still other seeds will germinate in either light or darkness but do better in one than the other.

In this experiment you can investigate whether or not light affects the germination of radish seeds. You will need 8 wide, shallow trays. Cover the bottom of each tray with several layers of paper towels. Add the same amount of water to each tray—enough to make the towels moist. Sprinkle exactly 50 radish seeds on each towel. Cover the trays loosely with plastic wrap before placing four of them in a closet or another dark place. The other four should be exposed to light in a place where the temperature is comparable to the dark location of the other trays.

After 24 hours, remove one tray from each location. Be careful not to let light strike the seeds in the other three containers that will remain in the dark. Count the number of seeds that have germinated in the dark and the number that have germinated in light. Record your data. Then calculate the percentage of the seeds that have germinated while in darkness. Do the same for the seeds that germinated in light. The percentage germinated can be calculated.

$$\% \text{ germinated} = \frac{\text{number of seeds germinated}}{\text{number of seeds planted}} \times 100$$

[FIGURE 5]

The data for the percentage of radish seeds germinated over a period of time in darkness and in light can be plotted on a graph like this. Use one color to plot the data for germination in darkness and another color for data representing seeds germinated in light.

Repeat the procedure on the next three successive days. Plot your results on a sheet of graph paper after drawing and labeling axes similar to those in Figure 5. Use two pens of different color to plot your data. What, if anything, can you conclude about the effect of light on the germination of radish seeds? Does light seem to help or hinder their germination?

EXPLORING ON YOUR OWN

Design an experiment to see what effect light of different colors has on the germination of radish seeds. What effect does colored light have on the germination of other seeds?

● 2.7 Bean Seeds Without Cotyledons: Can They Grow?

Materials: ✎

- lima bean seeds
- water
- glass
- teaspoon
- sugar
- 5 plastic cups
- salt
- honey
- paper towels
- 5 wide plastic containers about one-liter (quart) capacity
- cardboard or plastic
- labels (masking tape can be used)
- starch
- clear plastic wrap

You know that bean seeds use the food stored in their cotyledons to germinate and grow. But suppose a bean seed loses its cotyledons—can it still grow?

The answer may be that it can grow if we supply a substitute for the food that was stored in the cotyledons. To test that idea, you will need to remove the embryos from about three dozen lima bean seeds that have soaked in water overnight.

Before you begin that operation, prepare a solution by dissolving about a teaspoonful of sugar in a plastic cup (6.8 oz) nearly filled with water. In the same way, prepare a solution of salt and another of honey. Fill two additional cups with plain water.

Next, fold paper towels to fit on the bottoms of five wide plastic containers. Pour enough of the sugar solution over the towel in one dish to make it moist. Keep the remaining solution to moisten the towel as it becomes drier. A small piece of cardboard or plastic can be used to cover the solution in the cup. If you write an identifying label on the cover and place the cup next to the container with the towels and seeds, you will be able to quickly identify the solution on the towel. Repeat the procedure for the honey and salt solutions. Sprinkle some starch on the fourth towel (starch is not soluble in water) and then add enough water to moisten the towel. To the last towel add plain water. The cups of water, like the solutions, can be identified by labels on the covers.

Now that the moist towels are in place, you can return to the seeds. Take a seed and peel away the seed coat. Then gently slide one cotyledon off the other. You can now see the embryo resting on the remaining cotyledon. To isolate the embryo, place your thumb at the embryo's center as shown in Figure 6a. Push gently to free the embryo. Don't be discouraged if you don't succeed on your first try. With a little practice you will be able to separate the embryos easily.

As you isolate the embryos, place them on the towels that contain the five different liquids (sugar, honey, salt, starch, and water). Try to get at least five embryos on each towel.

Cover the containers that hold the embryos and damp towels with clear plastic wrap (Figure 6b). Don't seal the wrap. It should be loose enough for air to reach the embryos. In addition to retarding evaporation, the clear plastic wrap will allow diffuse light (not bright sunlight) to reach the embryos.

[FIGURE 6]

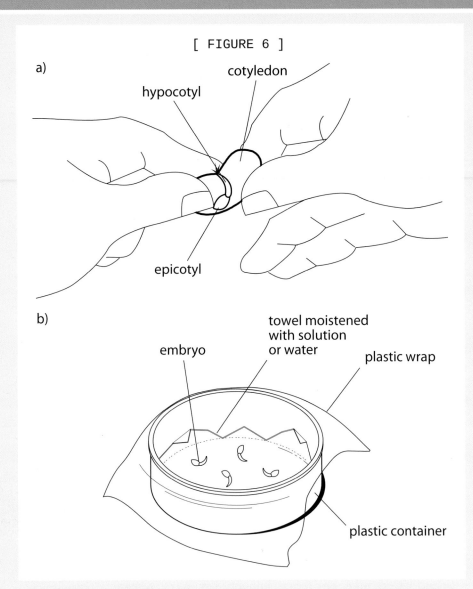

a) **You can remove a bean embryo from its cotyledons by pushing it gently with your thumb. b) The embryos are placed on moist paper towels in a container and covered with plastic wrap.**

On which, if any, of the towels do the embryos continue to grow? Which liquids seem to meet the nutritional needs of the growing embryos? For how long do the embryos continue to grow?

EXPLORING ON YOUR OWN

Plant scientists are able to grow mature plants from embryos like the ones you placed on different solutions. What do you think they have to do to make this happen? If you repeat this experiment by using just the solutions on which the embryos grow well, you might try carefully planting the embryos in soil after they have grown on the solutions for some time. Do you think the embryo plants will continue to grow after being transplanted to soil? Do they?

2.8 Seedlings and Their Cotyledons

Materials:

- 3 large flowerpots
- potting soil
- 15 lima bean seeds
- masking tape
- marking pen
- water
- ruler
- notebook

You know that cotyledons (seed leaves), which are the lowest leaves on the stem, contain stored food for germinating seeds. But do these cotyledons serve any purpose once the seeds have germinated and pushed through the soil? To find out, nearly fill three large flowerpots with potting soil. Place five lima bean seeds about an inch deep in each pot. The seeds should be spaced at least two inches apart. Number the pots 1, 2, and 3, using masking tape and a marking pen. Keep the soil in all three pots damp by adding water as needed on a daily basis.

As the young plants emerge from the soil, gently remove one cotyledon from all the plants in pot 1. Remove both cotyledons from all the plants in pot 2. Leave both cotyledons on the plants in pot 3.

As these plants continue to grow, observe them closely. Use a ruler to measure the heights of the plants in all three pots every other day. Also count and measure the size of the leaves on the plants in all three pots. Record your data in a notebook. On the basis of your observations and measurements, do you think cotyledons continue to play a role in the growth of young plants after they have emerged from the soil? What evidence do you have to support your conclusion?

EXPLORING ON YOUR OWN

If you cut off young bean plants at a point just above their seed leaves (cotyledons), will the plants live? Will they live if you cut the seedlings at a point just below their seed cotyledons? Design and carry out experiments to answer these questions.

Materials:

- 4 flowerpots
- potting soil
- sand
- peat
- gravel
- 48 bean seeds
- water
- ruler
- notebook

Does the type of soil in which seeds are planted affect their germination? To find out, fill flowerpots with different kinds of soil. Put potting soil in one pot, sand in a second, peat in a third, and gravel in a fourth. Plant 12 bean seeds about an inch deep in each pot. Keep the soils damp but not wet.

In which soils do the seeds germinate? In which soil do the seeds germinate first?

In those soils where seeds germinate, continue to water the growing plants with equal amounts of water. In which soils do the seedlings grow into mature plants?

Measure the heights and count the leaves on the plants in the various soils every other day until they mature (produce flowers). Record your data in a notebook. Compare the growth rates and the number of leaves on the plants in the different soils. In which soils do the plants thrive? In which soils do the plants die or grow poorly?

EXPLORING ON YOUR OWN

Try a variety of soils and soil mixtures other than those you tried in this experiment. How do these soils affect germination and plant growth?

2.10 Depth of Planting and Seeds

Materials:
- small stones or marbles
- ruler
- glass aquarium, clear two-liter soda bottles, or several wide-mouth jars
- sand or gravel
- potting soil or topsoil
- corn seeds
- water

Normally, seeds are placed in the ground to germinate because that is where they grow into mature plants. Does the depth at which seeds are planted have any affect on their germination and subsequent growth?

To investigate the effects of planting depth and seed orientation on seed germination and growth, place small stones or marbles about an inch deep on the bottom of a glass aquarium, several cut-off two-liter soda bottles, or several wide-mouth jars. Then add an inch of sand or gravel. The stones and gravel or sand will allow water to drain from the soil and keep the seeds from rotting. Finally, pour about eight inches to a foot of potting or topsoil into the aquarium or jars.

Place four or five corn seeds on the surface of the soil. Plant a similar number at one inch, two inches, four inches, six inches, eight inches, and deeper if possible. The soil should be kept moist but not wet. Orient the seeds in different ways (Figure 7), but be sure the seeds are visible through the glass so you can watch them to see if they germinate and grow.

[FIGURE 7]

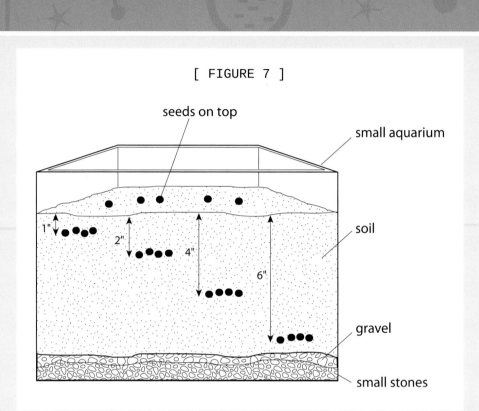

Does the depth at which seeds are planted have any effect on their germination and growth?

Does the depth that the seeds are planted affect the time it takes them to germinate? What happens if the seeds are upside down? Do the roots still grow down and the stems up? Do all the plants emerge from the soil and grow? What happens to the seeds on the surface of the soil?

Materials:

- thick cardboard to cover the surface of an old turntable
- turntable
- adult supervisor
- knife or shears to cut cardboard
- masking tape
- round pie pan or a long plastic dish (about as long as the diameter of the turntable)
- flat kitchen sponges
- grass or rye seeds
- water
- electrical outlet

When you ride your bike around a curve, you feel a force that seems to be pushing you outward. We call this a centrifugal force. You compensate for this force by leaning inward. You feel a similar force on a merry-go-round or a playground whirligig. Plants, of course, would experience the same force if they were growing on a merry-go-round. To see how they react to such a force, you can grow some grass or rye on a spinning turntable. The seedlings will "feel" a force that seems to be pushing them outward.

As you know from other experiments, roots grow downward and stems grow upward regardless of how the seeds are planted. Stems grow in a direction that opposes gravity, and roots grow in the direction that gravity pulls them. Can you guess how plants will grow on a spinning turntable?

To find out if you are right, **ask an adult** to cut a piece of thick cardboard so that it fits on the top of an old turntable and use masking tape to hold it in place. Cover the bottom of a large, round pie pan or a long plastic dish (about as long as the diameter of the turntable) with flat kitchen sponges. You may have to cut some of the sponges so they fill the space within the pie pan or dish. Add water to the sponges and then sprinkle grass or rye seeds on them.

Put the pan of seeds you planted on the turntable in a well-lighted location. **Make sure your hands are dry and then turn on the turntable.** The seeds will spin as they germinate and grow. Keep the sponges damp but not wet by occasionally adding water.

How do the seedlings grow after they germinate? Do they grow straight up? Do they grow leaning toward the center of the turntable? Or do they grow outward leaning away from the center of the turntable?

What evidence do you have that plants respond to centrifugal forces? Do they respond in the same way that you do when you experience a centrifugal force? What evidence do you have that the centrifugal force grows larger as the distance from the center of the turntable increases?

EXPLORING ON YOUR OWN

Design an experiment to find out how the speed of rotation affects plants growing on a turntable. Design another experiment to find out whether or not the plants grow differently if they begin rotating after they have germinated instead of before.

2.12 Sand and Seashore Sand

Materials:
- lima bean seeds
- 2 containers
- sand
- sand from the seashore
- water

Try planting lima bean seeds in ordinary sand. Plant the same number of bean seeds in sand that came from the seashore. Keep the sand in both containers damp but not wet.

Is the growth of the plants affected by the type of sand in which they are planted? If it is, can you offer a hypothesis to explain the difference? Try to design an experiment to test your hypothesis.

How is the germination and growth of other seeds affected by planting them in sand and sand from the seashore? What happens if you keep the sand moist by adding seawater?

Chapter 3

Leaves: A Plant's Food Factory

Leaves are the food factories for virtually all living things. It is the living cells of leaves that produce food, not only for the plants of which they are a part, but for all kinds of living organisms. Herbivorous animals, which, like all animals are incapable of making their own food, obtain their nourishment from plants. Carnivorous animals obtain their food by eating other animals. Although carnivorous animals eat other animals, some of the animals in their food chain eat plants. Omnivorous animals, such as humans, eat both plants and animals. But ultimately, all animals depend on plants for food. All foods used to nourish living organisms (except for a few species of bacteria) are ultimately the product of green plants.

Fungi—plants that lack the green pigment chlorophyll— are not able to make their own food from sunlight, carbon dioxide, and water. However, they too are ultimately dependent on green plants because they obtain their nourishment from dead organic matter—plants, or animals, the base of whose food chain begins with green plants.

3.1 Leaves and Light

Materials: ◁
-small potted plant
-south-facing window
-water

Place a small potted plant near a south-facing window where the sun shines in most of the day. Be sure that the plant's leaves face all directions evenly or are turned predominantly toward the inside of the room. Water the plant so that the soil in which it is growing remains damp but not wet. Watch the plant carefully over a period of several weeks. What happens to the leaves? How does their orientation change? Do they tend to turn so that they face the light? What does this tell you about the leaves?

Can you develop a hypothesis to explain why the leaves turn as they do? Can you design an experiment that will test your hypothesis?

3.2 Leaves and Veins

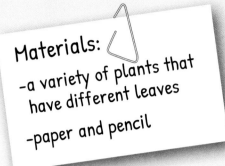

Materials:
-a variety of plants that have different leaves
-paper and pencil

If you look at leaves closely, you will see that there are lines running through them. Feel the lines and you will find that they are quite hard. They are called veins. As you can see, the veins all connect with the leaf's stem or petiole. The petiole is the part that connects the leaf's wide blade with the stem of the plant. Some leaves with different vein structures are shown in Figure 8. The veins, which lead to small branches and eventually to the main stem and roots, carry water and minerals to the cells that make up the leaf. The veins also provide a skeleton to support leaves and make them stiff. A floppy leaf would not offer much surface area to the light that the leaves need to manufacture food.

The way the veins are arranged (the venation) varies, but it is usually either parallel or netted. Leaves with netted venation have veins that branch off one another in various ways. Netted venation may be palmate or pinnate. In palmate venation, which is characteristic of maple and sycamore leaves, several main veins branch off the petiole like the fingers on a hand (Figure 8b). Leaves with pinnate venation, such as elm and wild cherry, have one main vein from which a number of side branches arise (Figure 8c). In parallel venation the veins run lengthwise along the leaf and are parallel to one another (Figure 8d). Such venation is characteristic of corn, iris, wheat, and grasses. Netlike venation is commonly found in plants with seeds that have two cotyledons (dicots), while parallel venation is common among monocots (plants whose seeds have a single cotyledon).

Look at the leaves you find on various plants. Draw the leaves and the vein patterns within the leaves. Which plants have leaves with parallel veins? Which plants

[FIGURE 8]

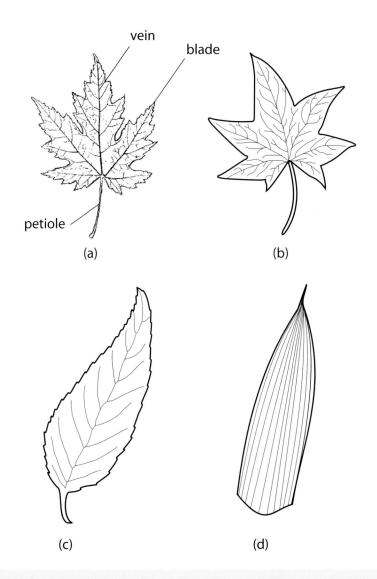

a) A typical leaf showing petiole, blade, and veins.
b) A sweetgum leaf is an example of palmate venation.
c) This wild cherry leaf is an example of pinnate venation.
d) Corn leaves like this one illustrate parallel venation.

have leaves with netted venation? Which leaves have palmate venation? Which have pinnate venation? What other difference do you notice as you compare the leaves of different plants?

Does the venation of the leaves on trees have any relationship to the structure of the bark? Is venation related to the color the leaves turn in autumn?

Materials:

- paper clip
- black construction paper or aluminum foil
- geranium plant
- adult supervisor
- gloves
- safety glasses
- tongs
- stove
- pan of boiling water
- alcohol
- small jar
- tincture of iodine

Leaves are green because they contain pigments that absorb most of the colors in white light except green. Because green light is reflected instead of being absorbed, most leaves appear green. One of the pigments in the cells of a plant's leaves is chlorophyll. Chlorophyll absorbs the light that provides the energy plants need to carry on photosynthesis. Photosynthesis is a process involving many steps by which plants convert carbon dioxide and water to oxygen and sugar. The oxygen that all living things need to carry on respiration is produced during the process of photosynthesis that takes place in green plants.

Because excess sugar produced in a leaf is changed to starch and stored, you can use the common test for starch (iodine) to confirm that food is produced in leaves when light is present. To carry out this test, you can begin by using a paper clip to hold a small folded piece of black construction paper or aluminum foil over both sides of a geranium leaf as shown in Figure 9. Be careful not to

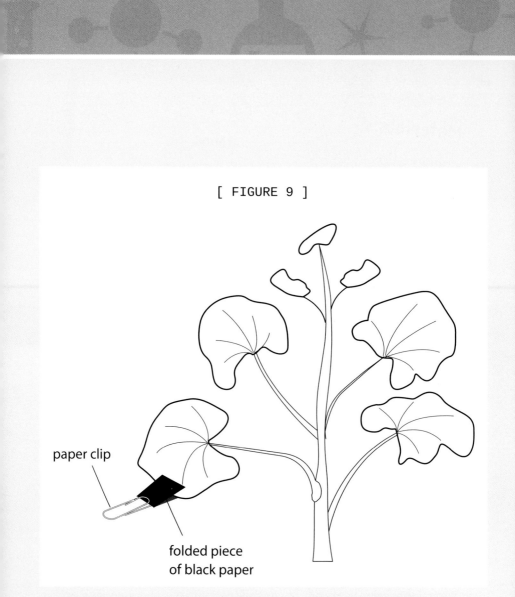

[FIGURE 9]

paper clip

folded piece
of black paper

A paper clip is used to fasten a piece of black
construction paper to a geranium leaf. Light will not
be able to reach the leaf cells covered by the paper,
but it will reach the other cells in the leaf.

damage the leaf when you attach the paper. Do this in the morning on a bright sunny day when lots of light will fall on the leaves of the geranium plant.

After four or five hours, pick the leaf from the plant, bring it indoors, and remove the cover. **Under adult supervision,** and while wearing gloves and safety glasses, use tongs to hold the leaf's stem so that you can immerse the rest of the leaf into a pan of boiling water on a stove. Hold the leaf under the boiling water for about one minute. The heat will break open cell walls within the leaf.

Next, you need to extract the green chlorophyll from the leaf. To do this, first turn off the stove because alcohol is flammable and should never be brought near a flame or red-hot burner. Place the now limp leaf in a small jar of alcohol and leave it overnight. The next morning you will find the alcohol has a green color due to the pigments it has extracted from the leaf. Mix together in a saucer approximately equal amounts of tincture of iodine solution and water, about 5 mL of each will do. **Remember: iodine is poisonous. Handle it carefully! Do not put it in your mouth.** Next, rinse the leaf in warm water before you spread it out and place it in the iodine-water solution.

You will see the leaf turn color as the iodine reacts with the starch to form a dark blue-black color. Notice that one area of the leaf is much lighter than the rest. Can you identify that region? In which area of the leaf did photosynthesis not take place? How can you tell? What evidence do you have to show that light is required for photosynthesis?

EXPLORING ON YOUR OWN

Design and carry out an experiment to determine how long the starch produced in bright light remains in the leaf after the leaf is placed in a dark place.

Materials:

- -4 test tubes
- -water
- -masking tape
- -marking pen
- -bromthymol blue solution
- -drinking straw
- -sprigs of elodea
- -4 rubber stoppers that fit test tubes
- -4 glasses or beakers
- -lightbulb
- -dark room or closet

During photosynthesis plants combine carbon dioxide and water in the presence of light to produce food and oxygen. The food is either stored by the plant or used as an energy source. (Plants, like you, use food as a source of energy.) The process by which energy is obtained from food is called respiration. During respiration, food is oxidized; that is, the food combines with oxygen in a complicated series of chemical reactions. The end products of respiration are carbon dioxide and water, the very same chemicals that are combined to make food during photosynthesis. But only green plants can manufacture food, and they can do so only in the presence of light.

With all this information in mind, fill four test tubes about halfway with water. Place a small piece of masking tape on each tube and label them 1, 2, 3, and 4. Add 1.0 mL of bromthymol blue to each tube. Bromthymol blue is an acid base indicator. It is blue in a base, such as ammonia, and yellow in an acid, such as vinegar or a solution of carbon dioxide. Carbon dioxide forms carbonic acid when it dissolves in water.

Using a drinking straw, gently blow air from your lungs into tubes 1 and 2. Continue to blow in air until no further change occurs. How can you explain the fact that the solutions turn from blue to yellow?

Place sprigs of elodea in tubes 1 and 3. (Elodea is a water plant commonly found in ponds or in stores that sell aquarium supplies.) Seal the openings of all four test tubes with rubber stoppers. Place the tubes in glasses or beakers of water near a bright light source as shown in Figure 10. Be sure the tubes are not so close to the

[FIGURE 10]

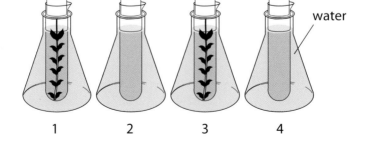

Sealed test tubes, two with elodea plants, are placed in containers of water near a light source.

light that the water becomes hot. After several hours, record any changes you see. Continue to watch the tubes for an entire day. What changes occur?

What is the purpose of each of the four tubes in this investigation? What do the changes in each tube indicate?

EXPLORING ON YOUR OWN

What do you think will happen in each test tube if the tubes are placed in darkness instead of in light? Test your predictions by repeating the experiment with the plants in darkness.

3.5 Growing Grass in Light and Dark

Materials:
- shears
- sponge
- 2 saucers
- grass seed
- water
- window or light source
- dark area such as a closet or under a box
- board
- green grass

Will plants produce chlorophyll in the absence of light? You can find out by germinating grass seeds in light and in darkness.

Begin by cutting a sponge in half. Place each half on a separate saucer. Sprinkle grass seed over each sponge. Then add water to the saucers so that it is about halfway up the sides of the sponges. Leave one saucer and sponge near a window or a light. Put the other saucer in a closet or under a box so that the seeds will be in darkness. Check each day to be sure that there is water in the saucers.

How long does it take before the seeds begin to germinate? Continue to add water to the saucers and watch the seeds. Do seeds germinate in both places? If they do, what is different about the two sets of germinated seedlings? Does chlorophyll develop in grass seedlings that receive no light? How do you know?

Here is another way to find out if light is needed for grass to produce chlorophyll. Place a board on some green grass near the edge of a field. (Obtain permission from the owner before you do so.) Leave the board in place, but look under it every few days until you can draw a conclusion based on what you observe. What happens to the grass under the board? What did you conclude? Remove the board when the experiment is finished.

Materials:

- geranium plant
- tweezers
- water
- glass or plastic microscope slide
- microscope
- clear plastic ruler
- graph paper

Pick a fresh geranium leaf from a plant. Turn the leaf so its lower side is facing you. Use tweezers to tear away a small section of the thin layer of tissue that covers the lower side of the leaf (Figure 11a). Carefully lay the tissue in a drop of water on a microscope slide as shown in Figure 11b. Add a cover slip and look at the tissue through the low-power lens of a microscope. You will see openings between the cells of the leaf. These openings, one of which is shown in Figure 12, are called stomates. Each stomate is surrounded by a pair of bean-shaped guard cells. The guard cells control the size of the openings. When the guard cells are filled with water, the openings are wide, and gases like oxygen can enter the leaf. When the guard cells lose water, they shrink and reduce the size of the stomates.

Count and record the number of stomates that are visible in the area seen through the microscope. Move the slide and count and record the number of stomates visible in the new region. Repeat this a few times and take an average of the number of stomates you can see at any one time through the microscope.

You can make a good estimate of the total number of stomates on the lower side of this leaf. To do so, place a clear plastic ruler under the microscope. Focus the microscope so that the millimeter lines are clearly visible. What is the approximate diameter of the area

Materials:
- small jar
- water
- cardboard
- clear plastic cup
- nail
- petroleum jelly
- small leaf from a shade tree such as a maple
- stone

Transpiration is the loss of water from a plant. The loss occurs primarily through the leaves where the stomates provide easy access to the air surrounding the plant. To see evidence of transpiration, gather together a small jar nearly filled with water, a square piece of cardboard large enough to cover the mouth of the jar, a clear plastic cup, a nail, clay, and some petroleum jelly. Use the nail to make a small hole in the center of the cardboard. Carefully remove a small but healthy leaf from a shade tree such as a maple. Be sure to include all of the leaf's stem (petiole). Place the leaf's stem through the hole in the cardboard. Then put the cardboard on the mouth of the jar so that the lower end of the leaf's petiole is in the water as shown in Figure 13.

Spread a thick layer of petroleum jelly around the rim of the plastic cup and around the leaf's stem at the point where it passes through the cardboard. Then invert the cup over the leaf. The petroleum jelly will form a seal around the mouth of the cup and the leaf's stem so that gases can't enter or leave the cup through its mouth or through the hole in the cardboard.

[FIGURE 12]

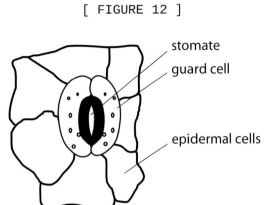

The lower epidermis (underside) of a leaf has small openings called stomates. The size of the openings is controlled by guard cells. Through these openings gases, such as oxygen, carbon dioxide, and water vapor, enter and leave a leaf.

Repeat the experiment for the upper side of the leaf. How many stomates do you estimate are on the upper side?

EXPLORING ON YOUR OWN

Compare the number of stomates on the leaves of different plants. Is the number of stomates per unit area approximately constant or does it vary from one species to another?

Do water plants have stomates on their leaves?

Materials:
- small jar
- water
- cardboard
- clear plastic cup
- nail
- petroleum jelly
- small leaf from a shade tree such as a maple
- stone

Transpiration is the loss of water from a plant. The loss occurs primarily through the leaves where the stomates provide easy access to the air surrounding the plant. To see evidence of transpiration, gather together a small jar nearly filled with water, a square piece of cardboard large enough to cover the mouth of the jar, a clear plastic cup, a nail, clay, and some petroleum jelly. Use the nail to make a small hole in the center of the cardboard. Carefully remove a small but healthy leaf from a shade tree such as a maple. Be sure to include all of the leaf's stem (petiole). Place the leaf's stem through the hole in the cardboard. Then put the cardboard on the mouth of the jar so that the lower end of the leaf's petiole is in the water as shown in Figure 13.

Spread a thick layer of petroleum jelly around the rim of the plastic cup and around the leaf's stem at the point where it passes through the cardboard. Then invert the cup over the leaf. The petroleum jelly will form a seal around the mouth of the cup and the leaf's stem so that gases can't enter or leave the cup through its mouth or through the hole in the cardboard.

🏆 3.6 Stomates

Materials:
- geranium plant
- tweezers
- water
- glass or plastic microscope slide
- microscope
- clear plastic ruler
- graph paper

Pick a fresh geranium leaf from a plant. Turn the leaf so its lower side is facing you. Use tweezers to tear away a small section of the thin layer of tissue that covers the lower side of the leaf (Figure 11a). Carefully lay the tissue in a drop of water on a microscope slide as shown in Figure 11b. Add a cover slip and look at the tissue through the low-power lens of a microscope. You will see openings between the cells of the leaf. These openings, one of which is shown in Figure 12, are called stomates. Each stomate is surrounded by a pair of bean-shaped guard cells. The guard cells control the size of the openings. When the guard cells are filled with water, the openings are wide, and gases like oxygen can enter the leaf. When the guard cells lose water, they shrink and reduce the size of the stomates.

Count and record the number of stomates that are visible in the area seen through the microscope. Move the slide and count and record the number of stomates visible in the new region. Repeat this a few times and take an average of the number of stomates you can see at any one time through the microscope.

You can make a good estimate of the total number of stomates on the lower side of this leaf. To do so, place a clear plastic ruler under the microscope. Focus the microscope so that the millimeter lines are clearly visible. What is the approximate diameter of the area

[FIGURE 11]

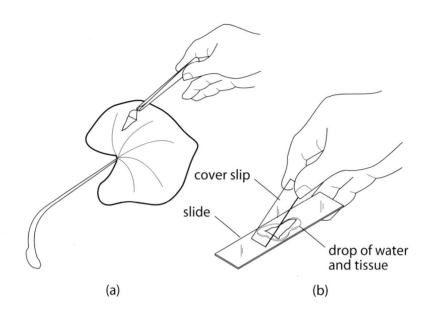

cover slip

slide

drop of water
and tissue

(a)   (b)

**a) Peel a small piece of tissue from the lower side of
a geranium leaf. b) Place the tissue on a drop of water
on a microscope slide and add a cover slip. Examine the
cells under the low power of a microscope.**

you see through the microscope? What is the approximate
area you see through the microscope? (Remember, the area
of a circle is πr^2, or $\pi d^2 \div 4$.) Next, you need to find
the total area of the leaf. This can be done by tracing the
leaf's outline on a sheet of graph paper. What is the total
number of squares on the graph paper covered by the leaf?
(You will have to estimate the fractions covered where the
edges of the leaf cover only a part of the squares.) What
is the area of one square on the graph paper? What is the
total area of the leaf? According to your calculations,
approximately how many stomates were on the lower side of
the leaf you examined?

[FIGURE 13]

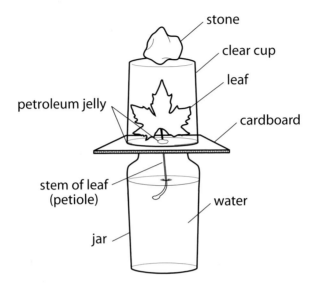

What collects on the inside surface of a container during the experiment?

Put the apparatus you have assembled in a sunny place. If there is a breeze, place a stone on the bottom of the cup to prevent it from moving. After an hour or two, look at the cup. What do you see collecting on the inside of the inverted cup that covers the leaf? How could it have gotten there? What do you think it is? What test could you perform to be sure?

EXPLORING ON YOUR OWN

Design and carry out an experiment to show that the water transpired from a plant's leaves is the same water that entered the plant through its roots.

3.8 Transpiration: A More Quantitative Look

Materials:

- 5 small coleus plants
- shears
- warm, sunny day
- water
- 5 clear plastic sandwich bags
- 5 twisties
- petroleum jelly
- balance (preferably top loading)
- warm, dark place
- electric fan

Obtain a flat of small coleus plants. The plants are probably in small plastic containers that are joined together. Use shears to cut through the plastic that joins the tops of the containers in which the plants are growing. Pick five of the plants that appear to be very similar in size and number of leaves and begin this experiment in the morning of a bright, warm, sunny day.

Water the soil in which the plants are growing. Slip a plastic sandwich bag over the container that holds the soil for each plant as shown in Figure 14a. Use a twistie to seal the top of the bag around the stem of each plant. Cover the top sides of the leaves of one plant with petroleum jelly. Cover the lower sides of the leaves of a second plant with petroleum jelly.

Weigh each of the plants on a balance (Figure 14b) and record their masses in a table like the one on page 78. After the weighings are made, the two plants with petroleum jelly will be placed in warm sunlight (Figure 14c). Of the

[FIGURE 14]

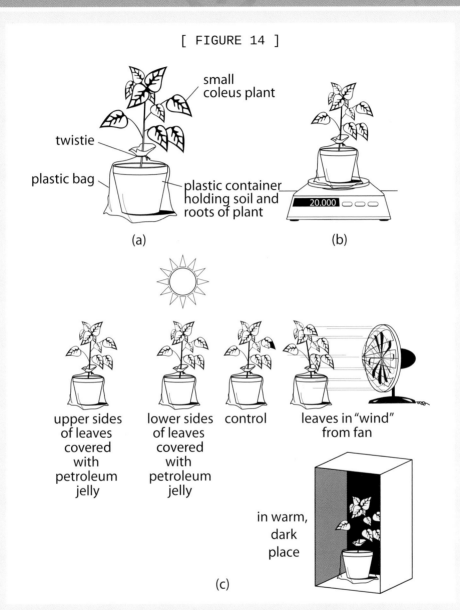

small coleus plant

twistie

plastic bag

plastic container holding soil and roots of plant

(a)

20.000

(b)

upper sides of leaves covered with petroleum jelly

lower sides of leaves covered with petroleum jelly

control

leaves in "wind" from fan

in warm, dark place

(c)

a) Select five small coleus plants. Seal the pots with plastic bags, as shown. b) Weigh each plant and record the data. c) After preparing the plants in different ways, place four of them in sunlight and one in darkness.

three remaining plants, one, which will serve as a control in this experiment, will also be placed in sunlight. A second will be placed in sunlight, but an electric fan will be used to provide a constant breeze (air flow) over the plant. The third remaining plant will be kept in a warm, dark place.

Reweigh each plant at two-hour intervals throughout the rest of the day. Between weighings return each plant to its assigned place.

At the end of the day, leave the plants in place overnight. Early the next morning make a final weighing of each one.

Which plant lost the most water through its leaves during the day? Which plant lost the least amount of water during the day? Two plants had their leaves coated with petroleum jelly, one on the upper sides of the leaves, the other on the lower sides. Based on the water losses of these two plants, are there more stomates on the lower or upper sides of leaves? What evidence do you have to support your conclusion?

What did you learn about the effect of light on the rate at which transpiration takes place? What effect does wind have on transpiration? How do you know?

Plant	Conditions	Mass in grams after						Mass in grams next morning
		0 h	2 h	4 h	6 h	8 h	10 h	
1	Tops of leaves coated							
2	Bottom sides coated							
3	Control							
4	In wind							
5	Kept in dark							

Chapter 4

Roots and Stems

A plant's stem has its origin in the epicotyl of the seed's embryo. Its root develops from the embryo's hypocotyl. When a seed germinates, the end of the hypocotyl, which is called the radicle, is usually the first structure to emerge. This first root's entrance into soil, following the force of gravity, enables the germinating plant to absorb water and minerals before the seed's supply is exhausted.

The emergence of the radicle is followed by the upward, gravity-defying movement of the epicotyl toward light and air. The stem provides the pathway by which water and minerals reach the leaves and other tissues. It also provides the support needed for leaves and flowers to develop.

A plant's primary root develops from the embryo's radicle and generally grows straight down into the soil. Shortly after the primary root begins its growth, it produces branches called secondary roots. The secondary roots grow horizontally as well as downward.

Materials:

- 2 small coleus plants
- brick or block of wood
- warm, dark place such as a closet
- cardboard sheets
- blocks
- tape

Place two small coleus plants side by side in a sunny place. Be sure the soil is damp and firmly tamped down. Then turn one of the plants on its side so it is horizontally rather than vertically oriented, as shown in Figure 15. A brick or a block of wood can be used to keep the plant above the ground, floor, or table. Watch

[FIGURE 15]

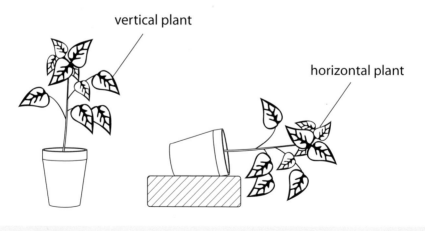

vertical plant

horizontal plant

What happens to a plant when it is turned onto its side?

the two plants over the course of a day or two. What happens to the plant that was turned 90 degrees? Does it continue to grow horizontally or does its stem turn upward?

Do you think the plant turned as it did because of its response to gravity or because of its response to light? You can find out by placing the same two plants in a warm, dark place for a day or two. This time turn the other plant so it is horizontally oriented. Leave the plant you turned before in a vertical position.

Does the horizontal plant remain oriented in that direction or does its stem turn upward? Based on your observations in these two experiments, do you think the stem turned because of its response to gravity or to light?

Do coleus plants always grow up in a direction that opposes gravity regardless of the angle they are turned relative to "up"? To find out, repeat the experiment you just did, but this time use cardboard sheets, blocks, and tape to build inclines that allow you to tip the plants at various angles, such as the ones shown in Figure 16.

To avoid any attraction toward light, place the plants in a dark place. After several days in the dark, are all the plants growing in the opposite direction from gravity's pull? When turned back with their pots on a level surface, will these crooked plants return to their former upward growth?

[FIGURE 16]

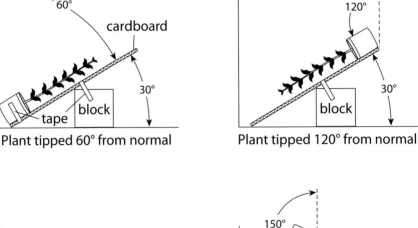

Plant tipped 60° from normal

Plant tipped 120° from normal

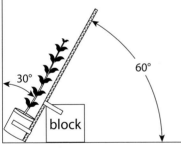

Plant tipped 30° from normal

Plant tipped 150° from normal

Will coleus plants always grow opposing gravity regardless of the amount they are tipped?

EXPLORING ON YOUR OWN

What can you do to produce a plant with a crooked stem? Will such a plant grow as tall as other plants of the same kind?

4.2 Upward Goes the Water

Materials:
- 2 fresh stalks of celery
- bowl or basin
- 2 drinking glasses
- water
- adult supervisor
- sharp knife
- cooking syringe (baster)
- red food coloring
- cutting board

Water is absorbed through the roots of a plant. To reach the leaves, it must pass upward through the stem. Once in the leaves, water is used to make food, but much of it is lost through transpiration, the loss of water vapor.

To see the path followed by water in its upward movement through a plant, you will need two fresh celery stalks with leaves. One of the stalks will serve as a control. Place this stalk in a bowl or basin of water. **Under adult supervision**, use a sharp knife to cut away the lowermost part of the stalk while it is under water. The cutting is done under water so that air bubbles cannot enter the stem. If they do, they break the column of water that moves from stem to leaves. Next, put a drinking glass in the bowl or basin and transfer the celery stalk under water into the glass.

Repeat the experiment with a second stalk of celery. Use a kitchen syringe (baster) to remove all but about 3 to 4 cm of water from both glasses. To the water surrounding the second stalk add enough red food coloring to make the water very dark. Leave the stalks for several hours. Check periodically until you see evidence of the red food coloring in the veins of the celery

[FIGURE 17]

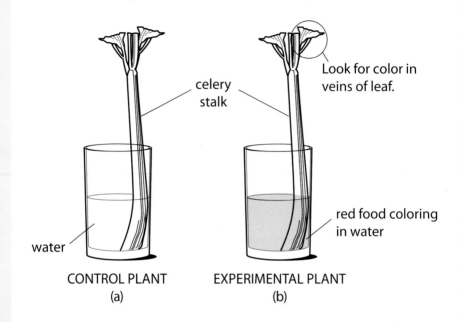

celery stalk

Look for color in veins of leaf.

red food coloring in water

water

CONTROL PLANT
(a)

EXPERIMENTAL PLANT
(b)

Celery stalks can be used to detect the upward movement of water in the stem of a plant.

leaves (Figure 17). While the veins may not appear to be distinctly red, they will be noticeably different from those in the control where colorless water was used.

Once you have detected the presence of food coloring in the veins of the experimental stalk, you can remove it from the water and place it on a cutting board. **Under adult supervision**, use the sharp knife to cut the stalk about 3 cm (1 in) above its lower end. Can you see where the red food coloring has moved up the stem?

Continue to cut the stem at 3-cm intervals. Can you follow the path of the colored water up the stem? Continue to cut all the way to the leaves. Can you find evidence showing that the colored water entered the short stems (petioles) leading to the leaves? Using a magnifying lens, can you find evidence that the colored water entered the veins of the leaves?

You can apply what you have learned by making a "Fourth of July" bouquet. To make the bouquet, find some white, long-stemmed flowers commonly known as Queen Anne's lace. Pick six of them, cut the lower ends of their stems under water, and place two of them in a glass containing water to which red food coloring has been added. Place two more in a glass containing water to which blue food coloring has been added. Place the remaining two in a glass of plain water. Wait a few hours and you will have your "Fourth of July" bouquet.

Can you make a Queen Anne's lace flower that has red, white, and blue colors all in the same blossom? Can you make a Queen Anne's bouquet that would be appropriate for St. Patrick's Day?

4.3 Where Does Growth Occur on a Stem?

Materials:
- bean seeds
- flowerpot
- potting or garden soil
- ruler
- fine line permanent marker

Plant several bean seeds in a flowerpot that is nearly filled with soil. After the seeds have germinated and a young plant with leaves growing outward from several points (nodes) along the stem has emerged, choose one of the plants to study. Using a ruler and a fine line permanent marker, carefully mark the entire stem with fine lines 2 mm apart as shown in Figure 18. At two-day intervals, remeasure the distance between the lines. Continue to do this for at least two weeks.

On the basis of your measurements, what can you conclude? Where does growth take place in a stem? What additional evidence do you have to support your conclusion? If you hang a swing from the limb of a tree, does the height of the swing's seat from the ground change with time? If it does, how does it change?

EXPLORING ON YOUR OWN

With marker and rulers available, design and conduct an experiment to find out where growth takes place in a leaf. Does it grow only at the edges or only at the base or tip? Or does a leaf grow outward at all points?

[FIGURE 18]

stem with marks
2 mm apart

By marking a stem at 2-mm intervals, you can find out
where a stem grows.

Materials:

- corn seeds
- cup
- water
- paper towels
- wide, shallow tray
- plastic wrap
- ruler
- fine line permanent marker
- clear plastic tape
- thin stick
- 250-mL (1/2-pint) beaker
- warm place

Soak about twenty corn seeds in a cup of water overnight. Then place the seeds on some moist paper towels folded to fit on the bottom of a wide, shallow tray. Cover the tray with plastic wrap and keep the towels moist, not wet, until all the seeds have germinated.

From the germinated corn seedlings, choose one with a root that is about 2 to 3 cm long. (You can use the other seeds in the next experiment, Experiment 4.5, which you should also start at this time.) Use a ruler and a permanent marker to draw lines 2 mm apart on the root. Use a piece of clear plastic tape to attach the seedling to a thin stick. Place the stick inside a small (250-mL or half-pint) beaker or jar that has about 50 mL (2 oz) of water on the bottom as shown in Figure 19. Be sure the root does not touch the water.

Put the beaker or jar in a warm, not hot, place. After three to four days, remove the seedling and remeasure the distance between the lines you drew on the root.

[FIGURE 19]

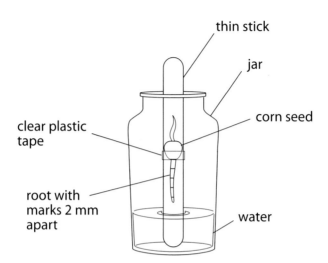

thin stick

jar

corn seed

clear plastic
tape

root with
marks 2 mm
apart

water

**An apparatus like this can be used to find out where
growth occurs in a root.**

On the basis of your measurements, what can you
conclude? Where does growth take place in a root?

EXPLORING ON YOUR OWN

Repeat the experiment with other seeds such as bean and
squash seeds. Is the growth pattern of their roots the
same as it was for the roots of corn seeds?

Materials:

- adult supervisor
- 12 germinated corn seeds
- sharp knife
- clear glass or plastic container
- moist sand
- masking tape
- marking pen

From the seeds you germinated for the preceding experiment, select twelve with roots about 3 cm long. **Under adult supervision,** use a sharp knife to remove 2 mm from the tip of the roots of six of these seedlings. The roots of the other six seedlings, which will serve as controls, should not be cut.

Half fill a clear glass or plastic container with moist sand. On one side of the container, gently insert the six seedlings, whose root tips have been removed, between the sand and the clear wall. The roots should be horizontal (Figure 20). Insert the six controls in a similar manner on the other side of the container. Then fill the container with moist sand. Use masking tape and a marking pen to label the controls and experimental seedlings.

Observe both sets of seedlings over a period of a week. Add water if necessary to keep the sand moist. Do the roots that have had their tips removed continue to grow? What about the controls? Does the direction of growth of the cut roots change? What about the controls? What can you conclude from the results of your experiment?

[FIGURE 20]

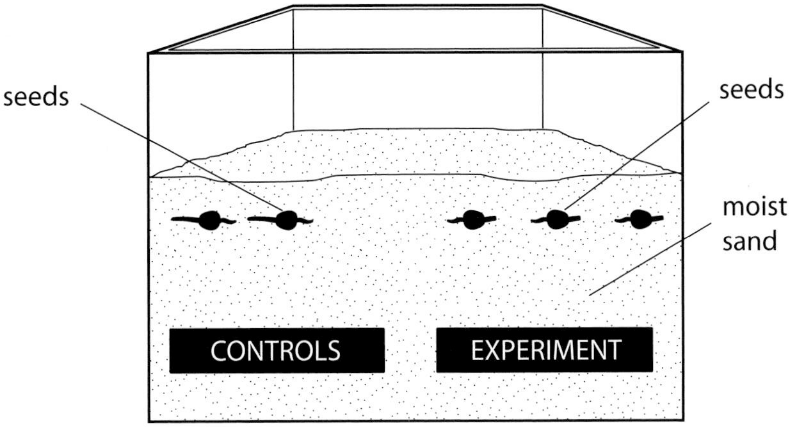

What happens to a corn seed if you cut off the tip of its root?

EXPLORING ON YOUR OWN

Repeat the experiment using other seeds such as bean and squash seeds. Are the results the same as they were for corn seeds?

Materials:
-radish seeds
-2 shallow cardboard trays, such as the kind used to package fruit in a supermarket
-water
-paper towels
-clear plastic wrap
-rubber bands

Line two very shallow cardboard trays, such as the kind used to package fruit in a supermarket, with moist, not wet, paper towels. Place about a dozen radish seeds on the moist towels in each tray. Cover both trays with clear plastic wrap and secure the wrap firmly against the seeds with rubber bands as shown in Figure 21. Set the trays on edge so that the seeds have very definite up and down directions.

When the seeds have germinated and you can see that their roots are growing downward and their stems upward, turn one of the trays 180 degrees (upside down). Leave the other tray as a control.

Observe the seedlings for several days. What happens to the roots and stems in the tray that has been turned upside down? What happens to the roots and stems in the tray that serves as a control? How do roots and stems respond to gravity?

[FIGURE 21]

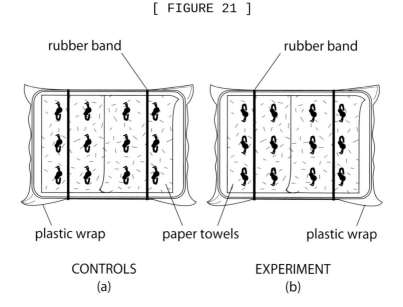

rubber band   rubber band

plastic wrap   paper towels   plastic wrap

CONTROLS   EXPERIMENT
(a)   (b)

What happens when seedlings are turned upside down?
a) Controls are left to grow undisturbed.
b) Experimental seedlings are inverted after
germination.

EXPLORING ON YOUR OWN

Design an experiment to find out whether or not roots
and stems lose their ability to respond to gravity
over time.

4.7 Twigs and Buds

Materials:

- deciduous trees, especially maples and willows
- sharp pruning clippers
- field guide book for trees and bushes
- marking pen
- masking tape
- tweezers (forceps)
- magnifying glass (convex lens)
- ruler
- adult supervisor
- containers to hold and support twigs
- water
- warm, sunny place

Deciduous trees shed their leaves in the fall, when the hours of daylight diminish, and spend part of the year without their green "coats." Despite their naked look, these plants have new leaves ready and waiting for the onset of longer days. These new leaves are inside buds. You can find buds like the ones in Figure 22. To study these buds more closely, you can collect twigs from a variety of trees. Be sure to ask permission of whoever owns the trees before you do so.

Under adult supervision, cut the twigs with pruning clippers. A field guide (book) for trees and bushes will help you identify any plants that you don't recognize without their leaves. Cut several small twigs from each kind of tree. Use a marking pen to write the name of the tree on a piece of masking tape. Wrap the label around the twig so that you can identify it later.

Once you have gathered and identified some twigs, take them indoors to examine them more closely. With a pair of tweezers (forceps), peel away some of the brown scales

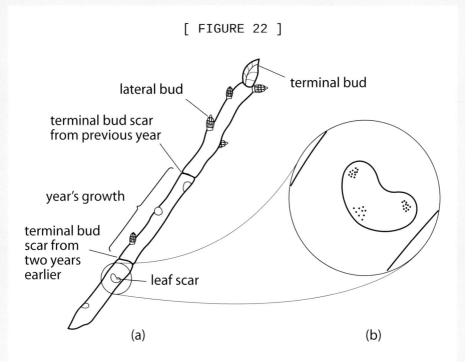

[FIGURE 22]

lateral bud

terminal bud

terminal bud scar
from previous year

year's growth

terminal bud
scar from
two years
earlier

leaf scar

(a)

(b)

a) A twig is shown with its buds and its leaf and terminal bud scars. b) The drawing shows an enlarged leaf scar.

from a terminal bud (one at the end of a twig). You should be able to see tiny leaves inside. Use a magnifying glass (convex lens) to examine the buds and baby leaves more closely. Can you find terminal buds (Figure 22a)? Can you find lateral buds? The distance between terminal bud scars is the growth that occurs from one year to the next. How much did each twig grow during the past year?

Return to the trees from which you cut the twigs. Look closely at the terminal buds on their twigs and branches. How much does growth vary from year to year? Can you find evidence of a recent drought?

Use the magnifier to look at the leaf scars (Figure 22b) on the sides of the twigs. The scars were made when leaves that grew from the twig during previous years fell off. Notice the small dots within each scar. The dots reveal where vessels that carried water, food, and minerals up from the roots and through the stem entered the leaf's petiole (stem). Some of these scars, especially the ones on horse chestnut trees, look like "faces."

Ask an adult to fill a sink with water and cut off the lower 3 cm (1 in) of the twigs under water so that air doesn't enter the vessels in the stems. Place a vase or other vessel under the water and insert the cut ends of the twigs. Remove the twigs and their container and put them in a warm, sunny place. Many of the buds, especially those from maples and willows, will open after a few days. It's a good idea to cut off another centimeter (1/2 in) from the bottom of the twigs once a week. A clean cut will allow water to enter the stem more easily. On which twigs do the buds open? Is the terminal bud more likely to open than the lateral buds?

Chapter 5

FLOWERS

Flowers are often so beautiful that we forget their role in the life of plants. It is within flowers that seeds are formed. Many people lose interest in a plant after its flowers fade and wither, but flowers are only one phase in the life cycle of a plant. The beauty and fragrance associated with many flowers were not designed to please people but to attract insects. For it is on the bodies of insects that pollen is often carried from one flower to another. The pollen contains the plants' sperm cells that will combine with the eggs buried deep within a flower and give rise to seeds and the next generation of plants.

There are two types of flowering plants or angiosperms—dicotyledonous plants (dicots) and monocotyledonous plants (monocots). Dicots, as you might guess from your experiments with seeds, have two cotyledons in their seeds, while monocots produce seeds with a single cotyledon. There are other general differences too. The leaves of dicots usually have veins that form a network, such as the veins in the leaves of maple trees or bean plants. Monocot leaves usually have veins that are parallel, such as the leaves of corn plants and grasses. The flower parts of dicots usually come in fours or fives or multiples of four or five, whereas monocot flower parts appear as threes or multiples of three.

The parts of a typical flower are shown in Figure 23a. The sepals are the outermost parts of a flower. They are often green and leaflike; however, in some flowers, such as tulips and lilies, the sepals are often the same color as the petals. Sepals protect and cover young flowers before they open. Petals are usually the bright, colorful part of a flower that lie just inside, and often between, the sepals. Sepals and petals are called the accessory parts of a flower because they are not directly involved in producing seeds.

The essential parts of the flower, which are needed to produce seeds, are the stamens and the pistils. The stamens consist of long slender filaments that have little knobs at their ends called anthers. It is on the anthers that you will find the very fine grains of pollen. If you rub your finger across an anther, you may be able to see some of the fine yellow dustlike particles of pollen. Perhaps you can collect enough pollen to look at it under a microscope.

The pistil or pistils, the female part of the flower, are usually at its center. The tip of the pistil, which is called the stigma, has a sticky substance that helps collect pollen grains carried to the pistil by insects, wind, water, or gravity if the pollen comes from the same flower. A pollen grain produces a long tube through which sperm cells travel to the egg that is located at the lower end of the pistil as shown in Figure 23b. The union of sperm and egg produces an embryo that eventually becomes part of the mature seed. Flowers that receive pollen from another plant of the same species are said to be cross-pollinated. Generally, cross-pollination produces larger, healthier plants than does self-pollination, in which pollen from a flower's stamens falls on the pistil of the same flower. Two ways that a plant avoids self-pollination

[FIGURE 23]

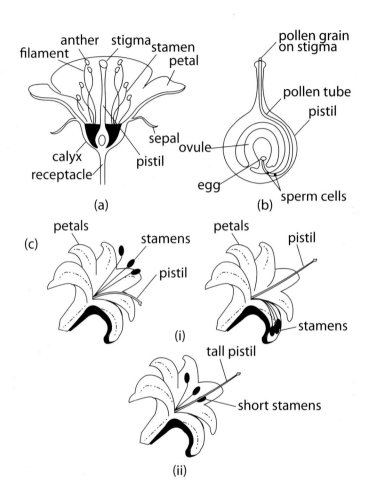

(a)

(b)

(c)

(i)

(ii)

a) The drawing shows the main parts of a typical flower.
b) A pollen tube grows down the pistil. Sperm cells
move along the pollen tube and fertilize the egg or
eggs in the ovule at the base of the pistil. c) Two
ways to avoid self-pollination include (i) maturation
of stamens and pistils at different times; (ii) tall
pistils that reach well above the same flower's stamens.

are shown in Figure 23c. Other ways of preventing self-pollination include having flowers with only pistils or stamens but not both on any one plant of a species (dioecious plants), chemical incompatibility between pollen and stigmas of the same flower, and a variety of structural mechanisms.

Insects are often attracted to plants with brightly colored petals. Some flowers have glands called nectaries that produce nectars, sweet liquids with odors that attract insects. Many people also enjoy the fragrance of these nectars. Bees, as you may know, collect nectar, as well as pollen as a source of food. The pollen that sticks to their bodies is carried from flower to flower with the insects. When their bodies rub against the pistil of a flower, some of the pollen sticks to the stigma.

Many flowers are small and drab. They have little color, no nectaries, and may even lack both petals and sepals. Such flowers do not attract insects, but usually produce an abundance of pollen that is carried by wind or water.

Flowers that have all four flower parts—sepals, petals, stamens, and pistils—are called complete flowers. Flowers that lack one of the four parts are said to be incomplete. Oat flowers, for example, are incomplete because they lack both sepals and petals. Anemone and clematis plants have stamens, pistils, and sepals but no petals. Willows produce flowers that have neither sepals nor petals. Furthermore, their flowers have either stamens or pistils but not both; consequently, willow flowers have only one of the four parts common to flowers.

Flowers with both pistils and stamens, such as tulips, lilies, roses, orchids, and sweet peas, are said to be perfect. In some plants, such as willow, oak, and cottonwood trees, the pistils and stamens are found in separate flowers. Flowers lacking either pistils or stamens are said to be imperfect. Flowers that bear only stamens are called staminate flowers. Those that bear only pistils are pistillate flowers. Dioecious plants produce imperfect flowers on separate plants. Such plants, some of which bear staminate flowers while others produce pistillate flowers, include willows and cottonwoods. Monoecious plants, such as oak trees and corn, bear both pistillate and staminate flowers on the same plant. The familiar tassels of a corn plant are the staminate flowers, while the silk found lower on the same plant is part of the pistillate flowers.

An oat flower is perfect because it has both stamens and pistils but incomplete because it lacks sepals and petals. Why are all imperfect flowers also incomplete?

5.1 A Flower to Dissect

Materials:
- flower such as a daffodil, lily, snapdragon, or tulip
- tweezers (forceps)
- paper and pencil
- magnifying glass

The best way to see the parts of a flower is to dissect a large one. A daffodil, lily, snapdragon, or tulip would be a good flower to dissect. If you can't find one growing at home, you may be able to obtain wilted ones free at a florist shop if you explain why you need them. Look at the whole flower before you begin dissecting. You can refer to Figure 23 on page 99. The green cuplike structure that connects the flower to the stem or receptacle is the calyx. The calyx is made up of the sepals, small, green leaflike structures that sometimes have the same colors as the petals that lie just above and inside them. How many sepals are there on the flower you are dissecting? Are they green or another color?

The petals make up the colored blossom that most people think of when they hear the word flower. How many petals does your flower have? Are the petals and sepals equal in number? Do you think the flower is a monocot or a dicot?

Use your fingers or tweezers to carefully remove the petals. You should be able to see the stamens and pistil or pistils found at the flower's center. How many stamens does your flower have? How many pistils does it have? A magnifying glass may help you see the parts more clearly. Draw a picture of the flower you have just dissected.

5.2 A Flower Hunt

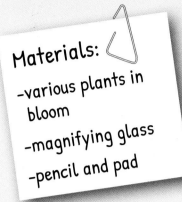

Materials:
-various plants in bloom
-magnifying glass
-pencil and pad

Examine a number of flowers, both wild and cultivated. They won't all be blooming at the same time, but you can begin to look for them early in the spring and continue to watch for new ones until the autumn. If your family grows indoor plants through the winter or if you live in a warm climate, you can continue your search year-round.

Early in the spring, you will find willows with their incomplete flowers. Soon, various other trees such as maples and oaks will bear rather inconspicuous flowers. Wild flowers, too, begin to bloom in the early spring and continue through the summer. Look for lilacs and forsythia during the spring as well as the beautiful blossoms of fruit trees.

As you examine these flowers, you may find a magnifying glass useful, although not essential. See if you can find the four parts common to flowers—sepals, petals, stamens, and pistils. **Be careful** as you do so because bees and other insects will be visiting these flowers more frequently than you do. With pad and pencil, make drawings of the various flowers and their parts. Be sure to label the parts and try to identify the plant on which they are growing.

How many of the flowers you find are complete flowers? How many are incomplete? How many imperfect flowers can you find? Which of them are dioecious? Which are monoecious? If you find pistillate flowers, can you find the corresponding staminate flowers? Can you find any flowers that are both imperfect and incomplete? Can you determine how each kind of flower is pollinated? Which ones appear to be self-pollinating? Which are pollinated by insects? For which flowers is the pollen carried by the wind? By water?

5.3 Flowers and Hours of Daylight

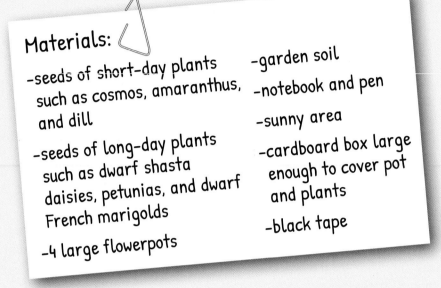

Materials:
- seeds of short-day plants such as cosmos, amaranthus, and dill
- seeds of long-day plants such as dwarf shasta daisies, petunias, and dwarf French marigolds
- 4 large flowerpots
- garden soil
- notebook and pen
- sunny area
- cardboard box large enough to cover pot and plants
- black tape

If you enjoy plants and flowers, you have probably noticed that different kinds of plants flower at different times of the year. Crocuses bloom so early in the spring that they may appear with snow on their petals. On the other hand, black-eyed Susans and daisies flower in the midsummer, while chrysanthemums, asters, cosmos, and dahlias bloom in the autumn. Plants that flower only when there is daylight for more than 13 to 14 hours are called long-day plants. Plants that flower only when there are fewer than 13 to 14 hours of daylight are called short-day plants. Short-day plants exposed to consistently long periods of daylight either will not bloom or will bloom only after a prolonged delay. Long-day plants exposed to short periods of daylight also fail to flower, even though they continue to grow.

Some species are indeterminate, or day-neutral. These plants, such as sunflowers, tomatoes, carnations, cotton, and dandelions, will bloom regardless of the period of daylight to which they are exposed.

In tropical and subtropical climates, within about 30 degrees of the equator, days are seldom longer than 14 hours. Consequently, most plants native to the region are short-day species. At latitudes more than 60 degrees from the equator, where days exceed 14 hours most of the summer, native species are long-day plants. In the temperate zones, between 30 and 60 degrees of the equator, both short-day and long-day plants are found. The short-day species bloom in the early spring and the late summer or autumn, whereas the long-day species flower in the late spring or early summer. Indeterminate species are widely distributed across the earth's surface. In greenhouses where the number of hours of daylight can be controlled, plants can be made to flower at anytime of the year.

When, and if, a plant flowers depends on more than the number of hours of daylight. They have to reach a certain size and be growing well. Plants growing in poor soils or extreme temperatures will not flower regardless of the period of daily light to which they are exposed.

To see how you can control the flowering of plants, you can perform the following experiment during the long-day season of the year. In the United States, that period is from about mid-May until early August.

Buy some seeds of both short-day and long-day plants at a garden store or from a seed company. For short-day plants you might try cosmos, amaranthus, and dill. Dwarf shasta daisies, petunias, and dwarf French marigolds can serve as long-day plants.

Fill four large flowerpots with garden soil. Following the directions on the seed package, plant about 20 seeds of a short-day plant in each of two pots. Plant an equal number of seeds of a long-day plant in each of the other two pots. Provide enough water to keep the soil damp but not wet in all the pots.

When plants emerge from the soil, record the date. After they reach a height of about 5 cm (2 in), remove any that are very small or very large so that you have about 10 to 12 plants that are very similar. Keep the pots in a place where they will receive the maximum amount of sunlight.

Since the experiment is being done during the longest days of the year (about 14 to 15 hours of sunlight), the short-day plants would not be expected to bloom. But you can reduce the hours of daylight the plants in one pot receive by covering it. Use black tape to cover all the seams and edges of a cardboard box so it is light tight. Place the box over one pot from about 6 P.M. in the evening until 7 A.M. the next morning. Repeat this procedure every day until the plants bloom. With only 11 hours of daylight, these short-day plants will be receiving the length of day they need to flower. How long does it take before these plants bloom? Do the short-day plants (the controls) in the other pot flower?

The long-day plants in the other two pots should bloom. How do you think you can prevent the long-day plants in one of those pots from producing flowers? Try it! Were you right?

5.4 Wildflowers, Height, and Season

Materials:
- ruler, meterstick, or yardstick
- wildflowers blooming from the early spring until autumn
- pocket calculator
- pencil and paper
- graph paper (optional)

From the previous investigation, you know that the time that a plant blooms may depend on whether it is a short-day or a long-day plant. The blooming of many wildflowers is also controlled by hours of daylight. You might hypothesize that the height of blooming wildflowers is related to the time of the year. Wildflowers blooming in late August, you might reason, will be taller than those that bloom in May because they have had a longer time to grow.

To test such a hypothesis, you can use a ruler, meterstick, or yardstick to measure the heights of blooming wildflowers from the early spring until the last wildflowers bloom in the autumn. At about the fifteenth of each month, from April until October, try to find five or more different species of wildflowers that are in bloom. Measure the height of at least ten different plants from each species. Add all the heights and divide by the number of measurements to find the average height of wildflowers for the month.

Plot your results on the axes of a bar graph like the one shown in Figure 24. You can use a different color for each species. Use a solid band drawn to the proper height to show the average height of wildflowers for each month.

[FIGURE 24]

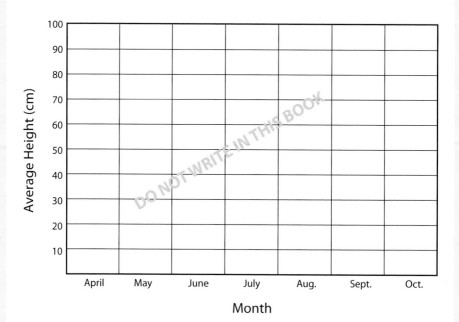

A bar graph can be made to record the average height of wildflowers each month of the year during which they grow.

After you have finished, you will have a visual means of representing wildflower height versus the time of the year. Do you think the graph will be the same everywhere in the United States?

Do your results support the hypothesis that wildflower height increases from the spring to the fall? Or do your results suggest something else?

Chapter 6

WHOLE PLANTS

This chapter begins with an experiment in which you will follow a number of plants through their entire life cycle, from seed to seed. While your plants are growing, you can also do other experiments involving the entire plant such as investigating the effects of crowding on plant growth, seeing how the amount of light they receive affects young plants, growing plants without soil, finding out how dandelions are adapted for survival, and repeating a famous experiment performed in the seventeenth century.

Materials:

-sunny area
-flowerpots or window boxes
-potting soil
-ruler
-pea and bean seeds
-large clear plastic bags or plastic sheeting
-sticks, dowels, or heavy wire

As you investigate the various parts of a plant, it is worthwhile to observe what happens to an entire plant as it goes through its life cycle. Bean and pea plants are fairly easy to grow and will grow to maturity in a reasonably short time (about two to three months). Seeds purchased from a garden-supply store have been treated to prevent mold from growing on the seeds. If you prefer to use seeds from a grocery store, you should drop the seeds into a solution that is eight parts water to one part bleach. After a couple of seconds pour off the solution. The solution will help retard the growth of mold, which can destroy the seeds. Plant pea seeds about an inch beneath the soil—two or three per pot is good. If you use a window box, plant the seeds about two inches apart. The same holds for bean seeds.

If you have an outdoor garden, peas can be planted in rows early in the spring, following the directions on the box. Beans should not be planted until after the threat of a frost has passed. Peas are normally planted in the early spring and require 60 to 70 days to complete their life cycle. For pea plants to grow, you need a sunny area.

Keep the soil damp but not wet. If the plants are grown indoors and the air in the room is very dry, you may want to build your own miniature greenhouse by using a thin plastic bag as a cover for each pot. The plastic will retard the loss of water but allow the exchange of gases between plants and the atmosphere. To keep the plastic off the plants, you may need to build a small frame from sticks or heavy wire. If you are growing a lot of plants, you can make a small "greenhouse" by draping plastic sheeting over a frame made from sticks or dowels.

Pea plants cannot survive hot weather; a hot room is not appropriate for their growth either. A cool or warm area, one that feels comfortable to you, will provide the best environment for the growth of pea plants.

Once the plants emerge from the soil, measure and record their height and the number of leaves on each plant every other day. After they are about 6 to 8 cm tall, provide each plant with a stick for support. Some plants may produce tendrils—curly growths that wrap around the sticks. If your plants produce tendrils, watch them carefully. Do all the tendrils wrap around the stick in the same way? If they do, do they curl clockwise or counterclockwise?

How many weeks or days pass before you notice buds beginning to form on the plants? How long before the first blossom appears? Choose one flower to pick and examine closely. Can you identify the various flower parts— pistils, stamens, petals, and sepals? (See Figure 23a on page 99.) Can you find evidence of pollen in the flower? On the stamens? Leave the other flowers alone so that they can go on to produce peas or beans.

As the flowers mature, look for them to begin to form pods. What happens to the flowers as the pods form? If you look through the pods toward a bright light such as the sky or a lightbulb, you may be able to see the seeds developing within the pods. **Do not use the sun as a bright light source. It can damage your eyes!**

EXPLORING ON YOUR OWN

You may want to eat a few of the peas and beans when they mature, but be sure to let some stay on the plants until the plants have died. Remove these seeds from the dry mature pods and plant them to produce a second generation of peas or beans. You might like to separate the seeds by size. Do large seeds produce larger plants than smaller seeds?

Watch the second generation of plants grow, blossom, bear fruit, and produce a new crop of seeds.

6.2 Crowded Plants

Materials:
-3 large flowerpots
-potting or garden soil
-ruler
-marigold seeds
-water
-warm, well-lighted place

People like their space. Most people do not like being jostled and pushed in a crowd. Even in one-on-one situations, people prefer to be at least a foot or two apart. How do plants fare in crowded as opposed to less crowded conditions?

To find out, obtain three large flowerpots that are nearly filled with potting or garden soil. Use the end of a ruler to make depressions in the soil about one-quarter inch deep. In one pot make the depressions about 1 cm apart. In a second pot the depressions should be about 3 cm apart. Make the depressions in the third pot about 5 cm apart. Place a single marigold seed in each depression. Cover the seeds by sprinkling a thin layer of soil over them.

Place the pots in a warm, well-lighted place and keep the soil damp but not wet. You should not have to wait many days before you see the plants emerging from the soil. Watch them grow over the course of several weeks. In which pot do the plants seem to grow fastest and mature soonest? Does the distance between plants have any effect on their growth?

6.3 Dandelions: Built for Survival

Materials:
- pencil and paper
- pocket calculator
- lawn with dandelions

Dandelions are, perhaps, the most familiar weeds in the country. They are as common to lawns as grass. In some cases, they have almost completely replaced the less rugged grass that home owners would prefer to see. The name, which means tooth of the lion, probably comes from the plant's sharp, jagged-edged leaves shown in Figure 25.

Dandelions are well adapted for survival. Their leaves, which can be cooked and eaten like spinach, lie flat and close to the ground, out of reach of the blades of most lawn mowers. Their long taproots, which defy the gardener's attempts to pull them from the ground, reach deep into the soil for moisture, so they remain green long after grass has withered in the dry summer heat. Their roots also store food so the plants can survive through long, cold winters.

Although you may not have eaten dandelion greens, you have probably tried to blow away the gray, fluffy seed heads that form after the dandelions' bright many-petaled yellow flowers have done their job. How are these seeds adapted for dispersal?

According to legend, if you make a wish and then use your breath to try to blow away the seeds, your wish will come true if you succeed with three blows or fewer. Do not count on it, however, unless you wish for a sure thing!

One of the things you may never have done is to count the number of seeds that make up the seed head of a ripened dandelion flower. Test your patience by making such a count now. You will be amazed at the number of seeds that form on a single dandelion flower head. Record that number. Then count the number of flowers on a single dandelion plant. Use the number of flowers and your count of the seeds to

[FIGURE 25]

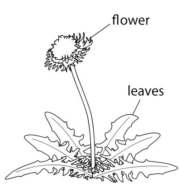

flower

leaves

Dandelions are as common as grass on many lawns. Some people eat the leaves of dandelions by cooking them as they would spinach. But don't eat leaves that have been treated with lawn chemicals!

calculate the number of seeds produced by a single dandelion plant. Assume each flower produces the same number of seeds. How many seeds are produced by a single dandelion plant?

Figure out a way to estimate the number of dandelion plants on a lawn. Use that number to estimate the total number of seeds produced by the dandelions on that lawn. What fraction of those seeds will need to germinate to double the number of dandelion plants on the lawn? How is their production of seeds an adaptation for survival?

Dandelions are sometimes called shepherd's clock. To see why, get up early and watch dandelion flowers early in the morning when they are struck by the morning sun. Continue to watch them periodically during the day. What happens to dandelion flowers when they are in the shade? What happens to them in the evening as the sun sets? What happens to them on cloudy or rainy days? Do you see now why some people call dandelions shepherd's clock?

Materials:

- red kidney beans or stringless beans
- glass of water
- 5 small pots or half-gallon cardboard milk cartons
- potting soil
- water
- totally dark place
- flashlight
- clock or watch
- 100-watt incandescent bulb
- ruler

How does the amount of light a young plant receives affect its growth and structure? You can find out by planting some red kidney or stringless beans.

Begin by soaking 30 kidney or stringless bean seeds in a glass of water overnight. Then plant six seeds about an inch deep in each of five small pots that contain potting soil. If you don't have pots, you can make some. **Ask an adult** to cut off the lower third of half-gallon cardboard milk cartons. If you make your own pots, be sure to punch a few holes in the bottom of the containers so any excess water can drain away. Nearly fill the pots with potting soil and add water to the pots occasionally to keep the soil moist, but not soaked.

Place four of the pots in a totally dark place where no light will reach the plants after they germinate. Ideally, this should be a place where you could go at night by flashlight. You could then turn off the flashlight and reach inside the enclosure to remove a plant for experimental purposes. If you place the four plants in a line on a shelf or floor, you can feel the pots in the dark and count them as numbers 1, 2, 3, and 4 from left to right.

Leave one pot near but outside the dark place. The plants in this pot will serve as a control. Later, they will be compared with the plants that will receive much less light. After two days water all the pots again. After five days, if the plants in the control pot are growing nicely above the soil, you can begin the experiment. If they are not growing above the soil yet, water the pots again and wait another day or two.

Once you know from observing the control that the plants have emerged and are growing above the soil, you can conduct the experiment. Place the control plants outside or near a window where they can receive light throughout the day.

Two days later, remove pot number 1 in darkness, seal the enclosure around the other plants, and then expose the plants in pot 1 to one minute of light from a 100-watt bulb that is 60 cm (24 in) from the pot. After one minute, turn off the light and place the plants back in the dark enclosure with the other three pots.

In a similar manner, expose the plants in pot number 2 to one hour of light from the same bulb at the same distance. Expose the plants in pot 3 to one day (24 hours) of the same light. The plants in pot 4 will remain in darkness throughout the experiment. These plants, having received no light, will allow you to see the effects of growing plants in total darkness.

After the plants in pot 3 have received 24 hours of light, remove the other three pots from the dark enclosure. Look at the plants in the four pots that were in darkness as well as the control plants that received natural light throughout the experiment. How do the plants compare? Which pot has the tallest plants? The shortest plants? Are there color differences among the plants? If there are, does the color seem to be related to the amount of light they received? Are all the plants growing straight up or have some of them curved? If they have curved, does the curvature appear to be related to the light? If it is, how is it related to the light? Have the leaves opened on all the plants? If not, is the amount they have opened related to the light they received?

EXPLORING ON YOUR OWN

Try growing plants in light of different colors. Do they grow best in red light? Blue light? Green light? Another color?

6.5 Hydroponics: Growing Plants Without Soil

Materials:

- bean seeds
- empty plastic gallon jug
- Epsom salts (from a drugstore)
- saltpeter (from a drugstore)
- household ammonia (from a supermarket)
- baking powder
- tap water
- wide, shallow container
- paper towels
- plastic wrap
- large, sharp nail
- thick cardboard
- clear 250-mL (1/2-pint) wide-mouth jars
- rubber bands
- clay
- chelated iron (from a garden store)
- plant food (from a garden store)

Although green plants can manufacture their own food from carbon dioxide and water, they, like all living things, need certain chemicals to live and grow. Normally, plants obtain these chemicals from the soil. However, plants can grow without any soil as long as they receive the chemicals they need from somewhere else.

Hydroponics, which means water agriculture, is the technique of growing plants in solutions that contain the minerals the plants need. Hydroponics allows growers to supply just the right quantity of various minerals to plants. Often soil does not contain the minerals the plants require.

To grow plants without soil you will first need to prepare a solution that will provide essential minerals. You can do this by adding about a quart of tap water to a clean plastic gallon jug or container that can be sealed shut. To the water add one teaspoonful each of Epsom salts, baking powder, and saltpeter. Finally, add one-half teaspoonful of ammonia. Seal the gallon container and shake it to dissolve the chemicals. Then fill the jug to the top with water, seal it, and shake some more.

Plants don't need the chemicals you used in preparing the solution, but they do need the chemical elements these compounds provide. They use the elements to make proteins and other necessary compounds. The chemical elements in the solution you made can be determined from the formulas for the ingredients as shown in the table below.

Substance	Chemical formula	Ions in the substance	Elements available in the substance
Epsom salts (magnesium sulfate)	$MgSO_4$	$Mg^{+2} + (SO_4)^{-2}$	magnesium, sulfur, oxygen
saltpeter (potassium nitrate)	KNO_3	$K^+ + NO_3^-$	potassium, nitrogen, oxygen
baking powder: a mixture of sodium bicarbonate	$NaHCO_3$	$Na^+ + HCO_3^-$	sodium, hydrogen, carbon, oxygen
and calcium biphosphate	$CaHPO_4$	$Ca^{+2} + HPO_4^{-2}$	calcium, hydrogen, phosphorus, oxygen
starch	$(C_5H_{10}O_5)_n$	no ions	carbon, hydrogen, oxygen
ammonia	NH_3	$NH_4^+ + OH^-$	nitrogen, hydrogen, oxygen
tap water	H_2O	$Zn^{+2}, Mn^{+2}, Cu^{+2}, Fe^{+3}$	hydrogen, oxygen, and trace amounts of zinc, manganese, copper, and iron

Soak about a dozen bean seeds overnight. Line the bottom of a wide, shallow container with moist, folded paper towels. Place the bean seeds on the moistened towels and cover the container with plastic wrap. When the seeds have germinated and have roots several centimeters long, they can be "transplanted" to the hydroponic solution.

Use a sharp nail to punch three holes in a thick cardboard square. The holes should be at the apex of a triangle that will lie just inside the mouth of a clear 250-mL (half-pint) wide-mouth jar that is nearly filled with the hydroponic solution. Punch a fourth hole in the center of the triangle so air can reach the solution that will be poured into the jar. Then thread the root of a bean seedling through each of the three holes in the cardboard. Place the cardboard on the jar's mouth. Use rubber bands to hold the cardboard in place as shown in Figure 26. Of course, transpiration will require you to add solution to the jar occasionally.

[FIGURE 26]

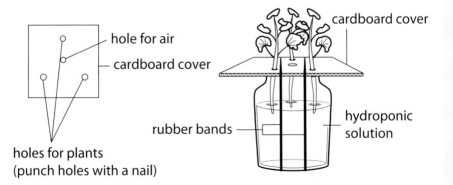

hole for air

cardboard cover

cardboard cover

rubber bands

hydroponic solution

holes for plants
(punch holes with a nail)

Plants can be grown without soil. The process is called hydroponics.

You can prepare several of these jars and place them under a good source of light. Should you experience difficulty keeping the plants erect, use clay to make small supporting sleeves around the plants' stems.

If the plants' leaves begin to turn yellow, they may need iron. You can buy chelated iron at a garden store and add a small amount to the solutions in the jars.

EXPLORING ON YOUR OWN

Try growing bean seedlings in ordinary tap water. What happens to them?

To find out what happens to plants growing in a solution that lacks one of the ingredients you used in preparing the solution—Epsom salts, baking powder, saltpeter, or ammonia—try growing bean seedlings in solutions that lack one of these chemicals. Can you see differences in their growth and appearance when compared with the controls growing in the original solution? If you can, are those differences eliminated when the plants are supplied with the original solution?

Try growing bean seedlings in solutions of various commercial brands of plant food using the concentrations recommended on the packages. Compare plants grown in such solutions with those grown in the hydroponic solution you prepared.

6.6 Van Helmont (1577-1644) and an Early Theory

Materials:

- 200 g of dry soil
- balance or platform scale
- aluminum foil
- large cookie pan
- potting or garden soil
- oven
- an adult
- plastic container
- radish seeds
- ruler
- water
- plastic gloves

Before the seventeenth century, people believed that plants obtained their food from the soil in which they grew. This idea, known as the humus theory, was tested in 1630 by Jan van Helmont. Van Helmont placed exactly 90.9 kg (200 lb) of thoroughly dried soil into a barrel in which he planted a small willow tree that weighed 2.27 kg (5 lb). Over a five-year period he added rainwater to the tree at regular intervals but nothing else.

Five years later, van Helmont pulled the willow tree from the soil, carefully scraped the soil from its roots into the barrel, and then weighed the tree. It had grown to 76.85 kg (169.06 lb). After thoroughly drying the soil, he found it now weighed 90.85 kg (199.88 lb). How much weight had the tree gained in five years? How much weight had the soil lost? What do you think van Helmont concluded about the humus theory?

After his experiment, van Helmont incorrectly concluded that the tree's added weight came from the water it had absorbed and converted to plant tissue. It was another two centuries before scientists recognized that green plants take in carbon dioxide as well as water and that light is needed for these plants to combine those two substances to produce food and release oxygen.

You can carry out an experiment similar to van Helmont's that won't require five years to complete. In fact, you can do this experiment in about one month—the time for radish seeds to grow and reach maturity. To begin, you will need about 200 g of dry soil. Weigh a sheet of aluminum foil. Then place the foil on a large cookie pan and spread about 400 g of potting or garden soil over the foil. **Under adult supervision**, dry the soil by placing it in an oven at 250° F for two hours. Pour the soil into a plastic container that you have previously weighed. Weigh the soil and the container on a balance. What is the mass, in grams, of the soil?

Estimate the number of radish seeds that you can plant in the container if they are placed 2 cm apart. Count out that many radish seeds and weigh them. What is their mass? Or is their mass negligible (too small to measure)?

Add water to the soil until it is damp but not wet, then put on plastic gloves and plant the seeds about 0.5 cm beneath the soil in the container. Be sure to scrape any soil on the gloves back into the container. Keep the soil damp, but not wet, as the seeds grow until they produce mature (flowering) radish plants. Once the radish plants are mature, remove them from the container being careful to scrape all the soil from the plants into the container that holds the soil. Pour the soil again onto a sheet of aluminum foil on a cookie pan and dry it as before.

While the soil is drying, weigh the radish plants. Then reweigh the dry soil. What was the mass of the radish plants? What was the mass of the soil? How much weight had the soil lost? Could the radish plants have obtained their mass from the soil? What do your results lead you to conclude about the humus theory? How does your explanation of the mass of the radish plants and soil after the plants had matured differ from van Helmont's?

Further Reading

Books

Barry, Dave, and Ridley Pearson. *Science Fair*. New York: Hyperion, 2011.

Connolly, Sean. *The Book of Totally Irresponsible Science: 64 Daring Experiments for Young Science*. New York: Workman Publishing Company, 2008.

Cook, Trevor. *Awesome Experiments for Curious Kids: Electricity and Magnetism, Forces, Plants and Living Things, Heat, Materials, Light and Sound*. London: Acturus Publishing Limited, 2012.

Margles, Samantha. *Mythbusters Science Fair Book*. New York: Scholastic, 2011.

Rhatigan, Joe, and Rain Newcomb. *Prize-Winning Science Fair Projects for Curious Kids*. New York: Lark Books, 2004.

Robinson, Tim. *The Everything Kids' Science Experiments Book: Boil Ice, Float Water, Measure Gravity—Challenge the World Around You!* Avon, Mass.: Adams Media, 2001.

Silvey, Anita. *The Plant Hunters: True Stories of Their Daring Adventures to the Far Corners of the Earth*. New York: Farrar, Straus and Giroux, 2012.

Van Cleave, Janice Pratt. *Step-by-Step Science Experiments in Ecology*. New York: Rosen Central, 2012.

Internet Addresses

All Science Fair Projects. *Botany*.
   http://www.all-science-fair-projects.com/category50.html

Science Buddies. *Plant Biology Science Fair Project Ideas*.
   http://www.sciencebuddies.org/science-fair-projects/
   Intro-Plant-Biology.shtml

Index